Caninestein

Caninestein

UNLEASHING THE GENIUS IN YOUR DOG

BETTY FISHER *and* SUZANNE DELZIO

Illustrations by Lou Powers

HarperPerennial

A Division of HarperCollinsPublishers

HarperCollins books may be purchased for educational, business, or sales promotional use. For information, please write to: Special Markets Department, HarperCollins Publishers, Inc., 10 East 53rd Street, New York, New York 10022.

FIRST EDITION

Designed by Helene Wald Berinsky

Library of Congress Cataloging-in-Publication Data

Fisher, Betty, 1938–
    Caninestein: unleashing the genius in your dog / Betty Fisher and Suzanne Delzio. — 1st ed.
       p. cm.
    Includes index.
    ISBN 0–06–273485-7
    1. Dogs—Training. 2. Dogs—Psychology. 3. Animal intelligence.
4. Games for dogs. I. Delzio, Suzanne, 1964– . II. Title.
    SF431.F57 1997   97–12179
    636.7'0887—dc21   CIP

97 98 99 00 01 ❖/HC 10 9 8 7 6 5 4 3 2 1

*We dedicate this book to those exceptional dog owners
who make a daily effort to provide their dogs with interesting lives.*

Contents

Acknowledgments

First, we would like to thank Lisa Ross of the Joseph Spieler Agency for encouraging us to pursue this project and for finding others interested in it. Two people who greatly aided our research efforts have won our enduring appreciation and respect. They are: Barbara Kolk, the Librarian at the American Kennel Club in New York City, and Guy E. Coffee, Information Specialist at the College of Veterinary Medicine at Kansas State University. We are also indebted to long-time trainers Janet Lewis, Carol Schatz, and Marjorie Hudson, who added their unique insights to this book. Finally, we want to thank the neighbors and friends who graciously allowed us to teach, challenge, observe, trick, hide from, and nag their dogs in our efforts to devise the tests, activities, and games herein.

Preface

Most dogs in America don't do their own brain cells justice. With all the elements they need to survive handed to them daily in a porcelain doggy dish, their minds get to go on permanent vacation. No challenges cross their paths. No new games inspire them to outsmart their owners. No duties allow them to shine. Potential Caninesteins are lost to endless boredom.

Although we adore our companions, we often don't know how to provide the novelty and challenge on which they thrive. We consider a walk, a game of fetch, or a long tummy rub adequate stimulation. Our dogs are capable of much more. It's up to us to provide opportunities that stimulate our pets' intellectual abilities. As authors, we hope that dog owners reading this book choose a few of the activities and environmental adjustments suggested and make them a regular part of their dog's routine. In fact, this book is a result of our own desire to provide interesting lives to our dogs.

Once you embark upon some of these activities, not only will your relationship with your dog improve, but his behavior will as well. A dog with an active mental life is more energetic and entertaining, and easier to train. A new game here, an environmental modification there, and you'll be amazed at how readily his intelligence comes alive and grows.

Caninestein

1
Measuring Your Dog's Intelligence

Dog intelligence? You may scoff. How bright can a creature that stares into garbage cans be?

Actually, our dogs are smarter than we think. While the average family dog is taught and responds to a mere three words, some dogs learn fifty or sixty. Although you'll probably never see a dog approaching you with a stethoscope and a smile, or even bagging your groceries, his intellectual capabilities are not limited to the scrounging and lounging that make up the typical pet dog's life. For instance, dogs who lead the blind have to learn when to ignore a command, if carrying it out would lead the owner in front of oncoming traffic or to any other potential disaster. That rejection of authority could not

occur without the ability to think in the abstract, evaluate different scenarios, and solve problems. How many of your coworkers go that far?

If you've always tried to convince friends and family of your dog's Ivy League potential, this book contains the tools you need. More than that, however, we hope that the resources here will help you provide a more stimulating life for your dog. The more the two of you interact in fun, positive ways, the richer your relationship becomes.

As you go through this book, keep in mind that it is tough to measure intelligence in any species. Wherever the subject of animal intelligence is raised, you'll find red-faced scientists with steam blowing out of their ears. The scientists we don't like claim that since dogs don't use language, they cannot think in the logical manner we do. They won't recognize that when a dog sees Mommy carrying a suitcase and immediately blocks the door like a linebacker, he's logically adding "suitcase" to "doorway" to come up with: "Must stop Mommy!" These uptight scientists hold that since a dog cannot reason like humans, it's ridiculous to attempt to measure intelligence using concepts designed for measuring human intelligence.

The cool researchers and we dog lovers have our own ideas about dog logic. The dog brings his leash to us because he's envisioned a future event: tugging us down the sidewalk while he sniffs a cornucopia of other dog smells. The dog gets his head stuck in the garbage can, then wags insanely all around the kitchen sending chairs and Tupperware flying to opposite corners of the room. When the can comes off, he's immediately under the table, cringing with guilt. He messed up, and he knows it.

We know that our dogs see cause and effect. When the leash goes on, he goes out. When he makes a big mess, he gets in trouble. It's similar to: when the paycheck comes, I go shopping. When the boss catches me balancing ten empty water cups on my head at the cooler, I'll soon be sitting in the big office trying not to scream.

No, we cannot ever get inside our dogs' minds and see the world as they see it. But we can know this much: a dog's brain and our brain are made up of the same materials. Not only do they have two hemispheres, a cerebrum, a cerebellum, and a corpus callosum, they also have the same regulating substances we do: serotonin, epinephrine, and oxytocin. Scientists accuse these substances, at least in part, for those feelings like love, gratitude, shame, and all the rest. In fact, in their book *When Elephants Weep*, Jeffrey Moussaieff Masson and Susan McCarthy make a strong case that because of these structural similarities, animals must experience the same vague phenomenon of emotion we do—at least to some extent. Likewise, if the structure and substances of a dog's brain come so close to ours, it's not unreasonable to assume that their thoughts—the product of that structure and substance—are similar as well. Here—much to your relief, no doubt—ends our scientific justification for measuring canine intelligence.

With that established, the next tricky question we tackle is whether some dogs intellectually outmaneuver others. This same question, when aimed at humans, elicits the wrath of mothers, teachers, and countless others. Getting an accurate measure of your dog's intelligence will depend on clearing up a few issues first.

While we hold that there is a range of intelligence in dogs that makes some smarter than others, we also acknowledge the possible obstacles in accurately examining it. Several variables may interfere with your dog's ability to respond to the challenges you present. Consider your relationship with the dog. Does he enjoy being with you and responding to your commands? Have you attempted to train him at all? Do you remember his name? His performance will depend on the strength of your relationship and the ease with which he understands your words and signals.

If you feel that your relationship with your dog has been neglected for a while, consider skipping the intelligence test for now. Go to Chapter 6, Games Brainiacs Play, and engage him in some of the fun activities listed there. Using gentle methods, try to teach him one of the household jobs we suggest in Chapter 7. After you've worked with him a bit, then attempt the intelligence test.

Your dog's level of attraction to food and treats will also effect his score in this IQ test. Since many questions involve food, if your dog is not food motivated, he may choose recess rather than test-taking. Don't give up too quickly. Usually, a dog only needs to find the right food to really get him excited. A lot of dogs turn their nose up at simple kibble. Treats such as liver cookies, hot dog slices, and bacon-flavored Cheez Whiz processed cheese spread are as irresistible to most dogs as dreamy Häagen-Dazs ice cream is to the most determined dieter. People who show their dogs swear by the miraculous powers baked into the Liver Cookie recipe here.

WONDER-WORKING LIVER COOKIES

1 cup flour
1 cup cornmeal
1 tsp. garlic powder
½ cup wheat germ
1 lb. raw beef liver

Put liver in food processor and liquefy. Add dry ingredients and mix well. On greased cookie sheet drop 1 tsp. of mixture and flatten with bottom of glass dipped in cornmeal. Bake at 350° 15–20 minutes. Cookies should be dry but not rock hard. Store in freezer until ready to use.

NOTE: If using a blender, cut the liver into 1" x 3" pieces and blend about ¼ lb. at a time. If you don't want to separate cookies by the drop method, you can also spread the dough in a rimmed cookie sheet. Cover about ⅔ of the sheet. Because the dough is very stiff, it will not run to the rest of the sheet. Sprinkle with cornmeal and bake. Cut into 2" squares immediately upon removing from oven.

Those dogs that are utterly bored by food become instantly motivated when a favorite squeaky toy is used as temptation (true for terriers in particular). In most of the questions in this test you can substitute the treat for a favored squeaky toy. And then there's the dog that will do anything for a freshly used tissue…but maybe we'll skip this grim group.

Fatigue and distractions are also score-squashers. A tired or irritated brain, human or canine, cannot kick academic butt. Try these tests at a time in the day when your dog seems energetic and alert. If you pick his most happy times of day (first thing in the morning or when you arrive home), play with him for five or ten minutes to take that frantic edge off. Test in a familiar area where no loud noises or unexpected events will interrupt you. The more ideal the conditions, the more ability the brain has to flex its dendrites.

Even if your dog is sufficiently food-motivated and the two of you enjoy a strong relationship, there is still his personality to consider. The overly dominant or overly submissive dog often cannot let his true potential shine through. If he is headstrong, he may blast through things, trying to boss the situation to his liking. As Dr. Michael W. Fox, noted animal behaviorist and veterinarian, explains in his book *Superdog: Raising the Perfect Canine Companion*, the dominant dog may not relax enough to evaluate that his attempts are failing. That he should try something else never crosses his one-track mind. The submissive dog, on the other hand, could be afraid of the equipment we suggest or of the unusual requests. Both of these dogs have

their endearing traits, so if you're frustrated with their scores, have confidence that you still have a valuable pet. For many of us, a submissive dog brings out our very best traits. Owners of dominant dogs find the same phenomenon. While he may never be able to score off the charts on an IQ test, he still adds much to our lives.

These exercises measure four components traditionally considered part of intelligence:

1. learning ability: how quickly can your dog retain and then retrieve new information?
2. problem-solving ability: when faced with an obstacle, how adept is he at surmounting the problem to win the reward?
3. memory: how long do objects he has seen or tricks he has learned stay in his mind?
4. language comprehension: how easily does he comprehend what you say?

Many of these exercises have silly choices, which are obviously intended to be ignored in scoring. The questions are in random order so that A is not necessarily the best or worst answer, etc. You'll find the scoring key on pages 26–28.

Because many of these questions are somewhat involved, don't expect to complete the test within days or even a week. Most dogs get confused when

bombarded with too many new requests at once. Use them as something to do with your dog from time to time. Jot down each score as you complete the exercise. At the end of a month, you'll have gathered the information you need to compute his final score.

Because of the limitations inherent in measuring canine intelligence, we encourage you to view the test as an opportunity to get to know your dog's personality and potential, and a chance to strengthen your relationship with him. That the test will help you decide which college applications to send for is only an added bonus.

IQ TEST

Learning Ability

1. A dog's learning ability can be measured in part by his accuracy in reading his owner's facial expressions. In a room where you typically hang out with your dog, take an object he is familiar with, but not crazy about (maybe an old toy), and put it where you can get it later. We don't want him to jump on it immediately. With the dog in the room with you, casually put the toy about six feet out to one side, halfway between yourself and the dog. Wait a minute without staring directly at the dog. Then, call his name to get his

attention. Once he's looking at you, shift your eyes to this object. Look back to him and over at the object several times. Does your dog:

A. Look at the object without getting up.
B. Go so far as to walk over and smell it or pick it up.
C. Stare back at you happily, close his eyes or look completely confused.
D. Yawn before drifting back off to dreamland.

2. Using methods that have worked for you, teach a new command, such as "car," which teaches the dog to jump into the car, or "corner," which teaches the dog to go to the corner of the room. (Of course you can always resort to "sit" if he hasn't learned it.) Guide him into this feat with gentle physical means—the leash or your hands—and food. Once he performs correctly, make sure to praise him with "good car/corner!" and give him a treat. How many times after showing him what you want does your dog know what to do?

A. 2–3
B. 4–10
C. 11–20
D. You'd rather eat the treat yourself than repeat the command.

3. Make sure your dog is in the room with you, but do not purposely attract his attention. Start when you determine that your dog is looking at you. At a time when you do not usually feed him, move toward his bowl and pick it up. Does your dog:

A. Open his mouth very wide and point toward his tongue.

B. Remain disinterested as you handle the bowl. He only gets excited once you've opened the food source and he can smell his dinner.

C. Watch you intently without rising OR refuse to move until you go toward the source of his food (the bag, the refrigerator, etc.). This dog may be smart enough to know you're bluffing. The important thing here is that the dog shows *immediate* interest. Signals such as perked up ears and wider eyes can tell you that he has made the connection.

D. Come toward you or his eating area immediately.

4. Tie a two- to three-foot cord around a favorite bone, rawhide chew, or pig ear. Let the dog see you put it on a table or piece of furniture that's at least twice his height. You might have to restrain him. We don't want him to be

able to jump up and snatch the treat with his mouth. Let the cord hang over the edge. Let the dog watch you pull the cord and get the bone. Give it to him and let him smell it, but take it away. Say, "get it," or whatever enticing words you use. Your dog:

A. Never gives up trying to leap on top of the table.
B. Leaps up at first and then paws or bites at the cord until the chew comes down.
C. Immediately takes the cord in his mouth or paws at it and is successful at getting the chew.
D. Throws the cat on top of the table and threatens to play with him if he doesn't knock that treat down.

5. Many studies have indicated that dogs are capable of "observational learning." The dog that has the opportunity to watch another dog learn something new before he's asked to perform the same task completes that task much more quickly. The dog that doesn't get to observe but must muddle through it by himself takes longer.

For this question, you'll need a second dog, a medium-sized cardboard box, a table, a two- to three-foot length of cord, a book, and a treat. At one end of the box, cut a door. Make sure the connected edge of the door is at the base of the box. The base of the box will be at the edge of the table so that when the dog opens the door, the flap can get out of the way of the rolling

treat. Put the box on the table, but lift one end by placing the book under it. The box is now tilted downward so that when the door opens, anything inside will roll out. Tape a three-foot cord to the door of the box, but make sure the door can stay closed even with the weight of the cord.

Now you will teach the first dog to pull the string which will allow a treat or toy to roll out. Using the cord, play tug-of-war with the first dog (for more information see Chapter 7). Allow the second dog to watch, but keep him contained. Don't let go of the cord at first. Then let go as the dog pulls, and the treat will roll out. (Dogs and people often learn through serendipity; this is the case in this trial. The dog will accidentally pull the string and release the treat/toy and then make the connection that he can reward himself in this way.) Encourage him as much as he needs.

Once the first dog makes the connection and pulls the string continuously to release the treat, remove him from the room. Set up the box and allow the second observing dog access. Let the dog see you put a big treat in the box. Does he:

A. Jump at the table and try to get at the box through physical means.
B. Seem completely clueless, unconcerned with the box.
C. Immediately pull at the string.
D. Appear interested in and work at the cord even if he doesn't succeed right away.

6. Another way to measure how well he's learned your social cues is to see if he responds appropriately to your moods. When you feel sad, does your dog solicit your attention and seem determined to lick you or touch you? If you feel angry, does your dog cringe away from you? Does he seem clueless? Does he even care? My dog:

A. Usually interprets my moods and reacts appropriately most of the time.
B. Is more clueless about my moods than my spouse.
C. Interprets my moods so well, I have to be careful because I don't want to upset him.
D. Has my shrink's phone number on automatic dial.

Memory

7. Make sure your dog knows the name of a particular favorite toy (bunny/ball) or buy a new toy and name it. Keep it in one place in the house or yard for a few days, allowing the dog to play with it and then to see you return it to that spot. When you give him the toy, say its name and give the dog a treat. Make sure he understands the toy's name and the difference between this toy and his others. Leave the toy alone for a day. The next day, go to the general area where the toy is kept and ask your dog to get it, saying, "get the bunny/ball" or just "bunny/ball." Does your dog:

    A. Look at you blankly.
    B. Search aimlessly around the area, never finding the toy.
    C. Take a few minutes to search, then find the toy.
    D. Run immediately to the toy's location.

8. Plan to put your dog outside of a room he commonly traverses for a day. Once he's outside, rearrange the furniture to some extent. That evening, after he greets you, does he:

    A. Seem frightened and cower as he looks at the room.

B. Immediately look at the room and seem alerted; wander about the room exploring, either tentatively or aggressively.

C. Respond as he always does, unconcerned with the new arrangement.

D. Look at and begin exploring the room after five minutes or so.

9. When a dog meets a guest for the first time in your house, he may be enthusiastic, but he's usually also a bit cautious. Invite someone the dog has never seen before to your home. Tell him to call your dog's name. Observe your dog's behavior. (Unless you have a really undiscriminating dog, he should exhibit some level of caution in the form of sniffing, cringing, or nervous movements.) Spend at least half an hour with this person and the dog, as you both play with and pet the dog. Encourage the newcomer to make a big fuss over the dog. Have the newcomer return to the house a week later and call the dog's name. Does the dog:

A. Fly to your friend and greet him as he greets someone he knows well.

B. Act exactly the same as he did when he first met this person—cautious? Nervous?

C. Proceed with a little less caution, but not quite as much enthusiasm as he shows greeting regular visitors.

D. Sneer and say, "Aww. You play with this one!"

10. Put your dog on his leash and have someone else hold him. At your dog's regular feeding time, fill his bowl and then put it in a room or corner of the yard that you never put it in. Lead the dog to the area, but don't let him get it. Lead the dog away from the area and from his usual eating area. Keep him occupied in another room for five minutes. Use treats to divert his attention, but just a few (we want him to be hungry). Take him to the area where his food is usually kept and release him. Does your dog:

A. Stop at his usual area, sniffing frantically for his dinner.
B. Run past his usual feeding area straight to the new spot you showed him.
C. Stop briefly at his usual area and then run straight to the food bowl.
D. Run helter-skelter around the yard/house looking for his food, taking a long time to find it.

11. Teach your dog a new command, such as "car" or "corner" as suggested above. "Corner" is probably the most convenient to teach. Say "corner" and then lead him to where you want him to go with food and the leash. You can use hand signals if you like to point to the corner. Make him sit. Reward with food and praise. After your dog has learned the command, practice it every other day. When it's so easy for him it's laughable, stop asking him to perform this. Wait for two weeks. Give him the command again. Does he:

A. Go immediately to the corner.
B. Continue to stare at you, ignore you or start barking.
C. Run around in an agitated way.
D. Roll over and play dead.

12. Object permanence refers to the dog's ability to realize that an object still exists even when he can no longer see or smell it. Puppies don't realize a hidden object still exists until they're about eight weeks old. For these little ones, when a toy or treat can no longer be seen or smelled, it's gone. Maturation solves this problem. However, sometimes a dog who has had a very limited environment as a puppy does not develop the necessary neural connections to establish object permanence. This deficit will hinder his response to life challenges.

To gauge your dog's ability to understand that hidden objects still exist, show the dog a new toy. He will be very curious to inspect it. Have your partner hold him on the leash so he cannot get it. Put the toy under a towel on the floor. Release the dog. After it has "disappeared," does your dog:

A. Run up to you or anywhere else, seemingly having forgotten the toy exists or look away bored.
B. Get confused and eat the towel.
C. Run immediately to the towel and try to get at the toy, successful or not.
D. Look around the area for the toy.

Problem-Solving Ability

13. Find a crate, wooden box or any structure that is strong enough to hold your dog's weight and high enough so that he cannot reach something on top

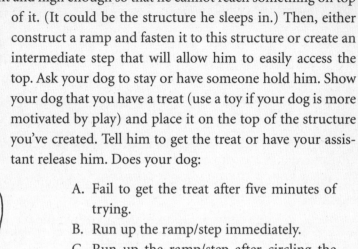

of it. (It could be the structure he sleeps in.) Then, either construct a ramp and fasten it to this structure or create an intermediate step that will allow him to easily access the top. Ask your dog to stay or have someone hold him. Show your dog that you have a treat (use a toy if your dog is more motivated by play) and place it on the top of the structure you've created. Tell him to get the treat or have your assistant release him. Does your dog:

A. Fail to get the treat after five minutes of trying.
B. Run up the ramp/step immediately.
C. Run up the ramp/step after circling the crate and jumping at it a few times.
D. Go to the Internet for instructions on a making a jet pack from rawhide chews and slobber.

14. Find a waist-high chain-link or wooden fence that your dog can see through. Make sure it has a door or opening. About ten yards down from the

opening, put your dog in a stay or have someone hold him. With your dog stationary, get his attention and then walk the entire length of the fence, making sure to pass the opening. Return to your dog. Climb over the fence and stand directly opposite your dog about twenty yards away from him. Call him to you. Does your dog:

A. Run straight for the area directly between you and himself, jumping, barking, and seeming generally disturbed.
B. Run back and forth along the closed portion of the fence in front of you.
C. Go to the area between you, spend some time there and then run to find an opening.
D. Run immediately through the opening without hitting the fence.

15. Get two cleaned tin cans (soup-can size). Put the dog on a sit stay or restrain him about five feet away from yourself and the cans. Place the two cans in front of you about three feet apart. Put a treat under the can to your right without letting your dog see it. (It's important that both cans smell like food.) Sit about two feet behind the cans facing the dog. Get the dog's attention, show him a treat and then quickly place it under the can to your left. After a wait of 15 seconds, release the dog. Does your dog go to the left can:

A. Directly, within 5 seconds.
B. Within 15 seconds.
C. Within 30 seconds.
D. After one minute or longer.

16. Tape a three-foot cord to a piece of cardboard. Turn it over so that the taped cord is on the bottom. Put a baby gate, screen or piece of glass (any see-through barrier) in a doorway that divides two rooms. Allow a space of three inches between the floor and the bottom of the barrier. Make sure the barrier is high enough that the dog cannot get over it. Put the piece of cardboard on one side, and run the string under the barrier so that at least one foot is on the other side. On the free end of the string tie a small piece of wood, preferably 1" x 3". You can also use a toilet paper roll—anything that will allow your dog to get a grip with his paw.

Now, bring your dog into the room. Have your assistant on the other side

put your dog's favorite food onto the cardboard square. Let him watch you pull the board to get the food to you. Guide his paw so that he does the same. Do this for three days. On the fourth day, does your dog:

A. Ignore the door, push against the barrier and put his paw and nose under it to try to get the food.
B. Pull at the board unsuccessfully.
C. Run around barking.
D. Pull the string and successfully get the treat.

17. Take a piece of food and let your dog see it. Put it under a couch, far enough where he cannot reach it with his nose and tongue. What methods does your dog use to get the piece of food?

ALMOST GOT IT! ALMOST...

A. He keeps banging his nose up against the couch without resorting to his paws.
B. He at first uses his nose, but quickly resorts to using his paws and nose.
C. Starts using his paws after a few unsuccessful minutes of trying to get to it with his nose.
D. Successfully eats through the couch until he reaches the treat.

18. For three days, put a treat under a towel and let your dog get it. Have a small box in the room at the same time. On the fourth day, put the towel where it's always been but put the food under the box. Say "get the toy/treat." The towel will smell like food so he will probably still check it out. How quickly does he stop this behavior that once rewarded him and try a different one?

A. Never. He searches that towel until he gives up.
B. Searches the towel for several minutes.
C. Searches the towel for a little while and then goes to the box.
D. Figures out there's nothing under the towel immediately and goes to the box.

Language Comprehension

19. Find two small saucers (or plastic lids) and a treat. Make the dog sit and stay in between the plates but two feet back from the imaginary line they would make if they were connected. You can also have someone restrain him there. Put a treat on each plate. Stand opposite the dog and get his attention. Say, "go right," point to the right with your right hand and lead him to the right plate. Do the same with "go left." After practicing several times (this may take a few days), put the dog in a sit across from you. With no hand signals or guidance, say "go right." Does your dog:

A. Gobble up a big pill bug innocently wandering by.

B. Run to you.

C. Go to the left plate.

D. Go to the right plate. (Don't worry if he runs to the left plate next.)

20. Name three different toys or objects. Your dog may already know "leash," "toy," "blanket." Put them in a line and then bring your dog to you about ten feet away from the objects. With the promise of treats ask for these items one at a time saying "get the leash," etc. Your dog:

A. Goes to or fetches the appropriate object 100 percent of the time.

B. Goes to or fetches the appropriate object 50 percent of the time.

C. Goes to or fetches the appropriate object 25 percent of the time.

D. Asks you to please spell it.

21. Teach the dog to jump over obstacles and to walk across a long flat board. If your dog is under fifteen months old he should not jump any higher than half the height of his front leg. Keep all your jumps dog-elbow height or lower while you are teaching him to jump. You can set up a board between four bricks for a jump or of course you can use agility equipment. For the walk, you can use an eight-foot plank that is at least eight inches wide. Teach the dog to jump with treats and praise. Use the commands "jump" or "over." Teach the dog the walk by leading him over the board with a treat in your hand in front of his nose, saying "walk, good walk" the entire time. (If you have agility equipment, you can set up any two obstacles to practice this with.) Keep your hand low so that your dog focuses on your hand and the board. After you're certain the dog understands the commands and which each refers to, you can start the test.

Put the two obstacles in the same plane about three feet apart. Place the dog about six feet behind the obstacles and make him stay. Go to the other side of the obstacles until you are directly in front of your dog but at least fifteen feet way. Choose one of the obstacles and then call him saying, "come, over!" or "come, walk!" depending on which obstacle you choose. Repeat this exercise five times. Does your dog:

A. Never choose the correct obstacle.
B. Come running to you without going over any obstacle.
C. Choose the correct obstacle two times or less out of five.
D. Choose the correct obstacle at least three times out of five.

22. When your dog is lying in the yard or in the house at least fifteen feet away from you, call him, but don't use the enticing tone you usually use to call him. It's best to do this when the dog is relaxing. Use a calm tone in the middle registers. Does your dog:

    A. Sit up immediately and look at you.
    B. Stay in the same position, but put his ears up and open his eyes.
    C. Snore even more heartily.
    D. Immediately come running.

23. Come up with a few names that sound similar to your dog's name. Dogs usually respond to the first syllable so calling him "Baloney" rather than his real name "Bullet" is likely to elicit the same response. Change the first syllable. See how discerning he is. Does your dog:

    A. Refuse to respond unless you get it exactly right.
    B. Look a bit alerted but fails to come unless you get it exactly right.
    C. Comes bounding to you no matter how far you get from it.
    D. Tell the cat you're calling him and laugh.

24. Most owners can put their dog in an excited state simply by using an upbeat tone of voice. The dog responds more to the tone of voice than the words. This time, check to see if he's got the actual words down. In a calm

tone in the medium registers, ask him if he wants to participate in his favorite activity: "Go for a nice walk." "Ride in the car." Does your dog:

A. Get excited even before the leash comes out.
B. Wag his tail and look a bit confused but doesn't approach you.
C. Jump all over you. He knows he's going out.
D. Continue to lick his paw, stare at the wall or drink water from the toilet.

Scoring Key

Note which group of exercises your dog was most adept at. Like people, dogs may be stronger in one area of intelligence than another. Some dogs may be great problem-solvers. Others are so good at language comprehension you know they were a United Nations translator in a previous human incarnation. Understanding your dog's strengths and weaknesses can help you make training adjustments.

1	A.	3						
	B.	4	2	A.	4	3	A.	n/a
	C.	0		B.	3		B.	0
	D.	n/a		C.	1		C.	4
				D.	0		D.	4

4	A.	2	10	A.	1	16	A.	1
	B.	3		B.	4		B.	3
	C.	4		C.	3		C.	0
	D.	n/a		D.	2		D.	4
5	A.	2	11	A.	4	17	A.	1
	B.	0		B.	0		B.	4
	C.	4		C.	1		C.	3
	D.	3		D.	n/a		D.	n/a
6	A.	3	12	A.	0	18	A.	1
	B.	0		B.	n/a		B.	2
	C.	4		C.	4		C.	3
	D.	n/a		D.	3		D.	4
7	A.	0	13	A.	1	19	A.	n/a
	B.	2		B.	4		B.	0
	C.	3		C.	3		C.	4
	D.	4		D.	n/a		D.	2
8	A.	4	14	A.	0	20	A.	4
	B.	4		B.	0		B.	3
	C.	0		C.	3		C.	1
	D.	3		D.	4		D.	n/a
9	A.	4	15	A.	4	21	A.	0
	B.	0		B.	3		B.	0
	C.	3		C.	2		C.	2
	D.	n/a		D.	1		D.	4

22			23			24		
	A.	3		A.	4		A.	4
	B.	2		B.	3		B.	2
	C.	1		C.	1		C.	3
	D.	4		D.	n/a		D.	0

SCORE:

Caninestein: 80–96 points
Definitely College Bound: 70–79 points
Average Joe: 60–69 points
Happy-Go-Lucky: 59 points and under

2
Living with the Gifted Dog

Like the class nerd that sniveled next to you in physics class, the gifted dog can get on your nerves. However, getting revenge by playing tricks and making fun of him probably isn't going to get you as far as it did in high school. Dogs like funny tricks, even if the joke's on them. The gifted dog figures out how to dig out of yards, sneak cookies, and arrange garden equipment into an obstacle course. He also becomes bored very easily. Training must be adjusted to accommodate his advanced skills. Otherwise, as occurs with his gifted human counterpart, the dog may choose to drop out, following his own desires rather than yours.

Since the whole subject of dog intelligence is such a sticky one, the sci-

ence of picking the Caninesteins from the great unflea-dipped has not been too aggressively pursued. While some dogs may seem "dense," their failure to be the Lassie you desire may be more a matter of personality. Many trainers find that the most easily trained dogs are not necessarily the smartest. Instead, these compliant pooches can have a very strong willingness to please and a clear idea that humans are the boss.

For some dogs, however, it's clear that their desire to please you cannot compare with their desire to please themselves. Give them a command and, if their favorite shows aren't on, *maybe* they'll respond. These dogs tend to be independent or dominant. On the other hand, shy dogs may be too distracted by their fears to make sense of what you're asking. Temperament more than intelligence influences the training job you'll encounter.

No one wants to hurt an owner's feelings by informing them that their dog doesn't belong in college prep classes. Nevertheless, you will hear a trainer now and then say, "This dog is smarter than Steve Allen!" or "That poor dog has the IQ of a rawhide chew." The few brave trainers and researchers who assert that some are more intelligent than others find that the Caninesteins of the bunch share the following traits:

1. Reluctance to repeat a game such as fetch many times.
2. Reluctance to repeat any training step many times.
3. A curiosity that can get them into trouble as everything must be explored.

4. Ability to accurately interpret an owner's mood.
5. Ability to quickly understand new words.
6. Ability to read owner's body language to their advantage.
7. Solid memory of new commands.
8. Ability to withstand distractions, to tune out things going on in the environment in order to concentrate on the task at hand.
9. Inability comb their hair straight or get a date for Friday night.

Why Your Dog Has the Smart Gene (Hint: You Had Nothing to Do with It)

If your dog participates in most of the above behaviors, you are hereby granted the right to dance in front of your neighbors' homes chanting in your best childish singsong, "My dog's smarter than your dog. I'm a genius for buying him." But true intelligence is rare, and your neighbors may want some background information to substantiate your claims.

How did your dog get so smart? Some people look at the parents of very bright children and ask the same question. It's tough to determine where intelligence comes from, but from the limited studies on the subject, it's clear that having intelligent parents, and a mother who's inquisitive as well can be a bonus for a young dog.

Intelligence can be passed on genetically. In fact, breeders choose for qualities like "maternal instinct" and "likeliness to react aggressively," both of

which are just as intangible as intelligence. Whether a breeder is deliberately looking to enhance intelligence or not, intelligent parents can pass that trait to their offspring.

Secondly, since researchers have found that dogs do learn by observation, a mother dog who is curious and explores new objects, people, and environments usually passes that behavior to her pups. Curiosity can be a great brain booster. A dog sees a mouse or lizard on the other side of a fence and learns quite effectively how to solve the problem of barriers. A dog approaches a hostile animal such as a skunk and quickly learns the ways of the wild. With each curiosity-inspired encounter, he adds to his storehouse of knowledge and forms new neural patterns in his brain. If your dog was lucky enough to have an inquisitive mother, the inquisitiveness he picked up from her will help keep his brain in top form.

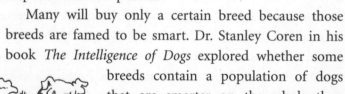

Many will buy only a certain breed because those breeds are famed to be smart. Dr. Stanley Coren in his book *The Intelligence of Dogs* explored whether some breeds contain a population of dogs that are smarter on the whole than those in other breeds. While his book was very popular, the owners of the dogs he had placed at the bottom of his intelligence ranking bought a bunch of torches and pikes and surrounded his

house chanting, "Bring out the monster!" (Actually, they wrote a lot of mean letters and articles in the dog magazines.) These owners felt he'd drawn erroneous conclusions from the statistics he compiled. For Coren, studying this subject through close scientific methods proved impossible. That project would have cost at least three million dollars and taken several years. He approached it from a different angle.

Coren established his conclusions by surveying over two hundred obedience judges. His questionnaire asked them to give their opinion as to which breeds they would rate as the ten most intelligent and which the ten least intelligent. He found remarkable agreement among the judges. The vast majority placed the border collie, German shepherd, Shetland sheepdog, poodle, and golden retriever in the top ten. Owners of those breeds that essentially flunked (Afghans, basenjis, bulldogs, Chow Chows) grumbled on the grounds that the judges were not making their determinations based on intelligence. Rather, the deciding factor was clearly a matter of performance in the obedience ring—a factor based on willingness to respond to human control. It's true: you don't see too many Afghans and their allegedly slower brethren in the obedience trials. Most Afghan lovers admit that these sleek dogs are tougher to train. But, whether this greater struggle results from lower intelligence or other personality traits is still open to dispute.

It's our conclusion that the breed does not the Caninestein make. Coren did write in his book that there can be brilliant Afghans, and border collies that were bimbos in previous lives. There may indeed be more smart border

collies than smart Afghans, but the strict determination of intelligence must be made on a case-by-case basis.

How the Smart Ones Do It

"Things just come so much easier to me," the nerdy dog quips before being slapped by his pack members. Observing how your dog handles a difficult situation can provide clues about his intelligence. When a dog (or person for that matter) is faced with an obstacle, the smart one surmounts it more quickly. He does this by using a variety of strategies. The slower dog has one solution with which it repeatedly bombards the obstacle. For instance, with a treat tucked under a couch, the slow dog bangs his nose against the couch's edge over and over, trying to reach the treat with that part of the body with which it's accustomed to handling food. Returning to the same response repeatedly is termed "habit fixation." The smart dog may try putting his nose under the couch, but upon failing, will immediately start using one and even two paws. The smarter dog's flexibility further enhances his learning ability and his effectiveness in responding to his environment.

Another good indicator of intelligence is a dog's propensity to reverse a routine or learned behavior when conditions change. If a quick-witted dog has learned that a piece of food is under a towel, and then someone throws a food-scented towel on the floor but puts the food elsewhere, he'll quickly explore the towel. Upon finding nothing, he'll move to other areas looking

for the food. The smart dog easily changes his behavior when that behavior goes unrewarded. The ability to reverse actions based on old, misguided ideas distinguishes him from the rest of his pack and from most Republicans as well.

Caninestein as Roommate

The biggest challenge involved in living with a bright dog is protecting your living quarters and property. His exploratory nature leads to escapes and vandalism, even crime. The Mensa Dog Society's charter (found in a Peruvian cave and dating circa A.D. 1145) reveals just why bright dogs seem compelled to turn a house upside down. It reads:

We will have our mind candy. To meet this end, we all commit to the following duties. We must dig up the ground to see where the bugs go. We must look into all toilets, waste bins, and washing machines on a regular basis. We must stretch and peer over fences to see what's there. We must approach and evaluate all strange noises. We must stand transfixed as we observe the menial activities of our humans— every turn of the screwdriver and brush of the broom must be closely monitored and noted.

We must bring all objects that lie on bookshelves and cabinets down to our nose level so that exploration and dissection be made more convenient. In our pursuit of knowledge, we must not concern ourselves with the objects that sacrifice themselves by being knocked over. We must actively strive to find new territories to run our noses over. We must find new friends to join us in our pursuits. We must consume crunchy balls of dirt, used tissues, pieces of cellophane, screws, beer cans, puffs of cat hair, all in hopes of furthering our knowledge of the natural world around us. Above all, we must ignore the boring. These duties are to be accepted with pride, bravery and joy, for we are CANINESTEINS!

The bottom line is: the intelligent dog has to get into things. Because of this propensity, take a few precautions before leaving the dog home alone for several hours.

1. Once all items in the yard or house have been investigated and cataloged, the dog will be looking for new areas to explore. If he stays in the yard while you're gone, make sure you have a six-foot fence designed so he can't dig out. Some dogs can climb chain-link fences, so be careful.

2. Make sure all the objects in his area are those he can investigate safely. Keep small objects out of his reach. Where humans check out a new object by picking it up in our hands, the dog does the same by pick-

ing it up in his mouth. Trips to the pet emergency clinic and calls to your homeowners' insurance agent can cause the dog to look less cute to you every day.

3. Bright dogs get bored. One of the ways they sidestep boredom is by making things happen. For instance, they especially like to make holes in cushy beds. Once they see that first piece of stuffing fall out, their life's work is revealed! Object must be eviscerated! Similarly, they may assign themselves the job of removing the trim in several of your rooms. Once they get started, the job must be finished. Once it is, another accomplishment! Bitter Apple™, a foul-tasting chewing deterrent, can put an end to this dogged determination to destroy.

Training Adjustments for Caninestein

As Roger Caras, author of *A Dog is Listening* and other insightful dog books, notes, bright dogs have so much they want to explore and discover, getting and keeping their attention can be a real struggle. However, making a few adjustments can help training go smoothly.

For fifteen years, Janet Lewis, author of *Smart Trainers; Brilliant Dogs*, has been training champion border collies—the breed placed at the top of Coren's intelligence ranking. When watching these black-and-white wonders work, it's tough to believe that the key to their success lies simply with their willingness to please. Intelligence obviously plays a big part. Trained border

collies follow very complex directions. (It's rumored that they don't even look at the pictures that come along with instruction sheets.) For instance, after rounding up the sheep and bringing the herd in, at the shepherd's direction they must turn and check the field for stragglers. Instinct makes them want to bring that herd all the way to the owner. A command makes them leave their route to gather the few missed and get them back before the rest of the herd wanders away. These rigorous tasks require concentration, ability to think in the abstract (imagination), and on-the-spot problem-solving. Most admit that border collies hang out on the top of the brilliance scale. Unlike many other breeds, intelligence is purposely bred for in these lines.

With all of these great attributes come the drawbacks. The ability to understand complex commands translates into boredom with simple ones. Janet Lewis must battle this restlessness constantly. In their obedience trials,

her dogs must perform a sequence of exercises at a distance from her. They are guided by her hand signals and must wait for each hand signal to proceed to the next exercise in the sequence. What she finds, however, is that once they see the first hand signal, they think, "Oh heck, I know this routine!" and tear through the whole sequence without waiting for her direction. Sounds impressive, but this behavior loses points in the showring.

When training your dog, keep these adjustments in mind:

1. Getting and keeping a smart dog's attention is probably the biggest hurdle the owner faces. To this end, make yourself the most interesting thing in the environment. Praise in an excited, happy voice. Happy dogs indicate their pleasure by wiggling. You should do the same. Move about when you're happy with their performance. Act excited when giving commands. Vary rewards from petting and praise to food. Vary the types of treats you use. Make sure that nothing else around can compete with how interesting and fun you are.

2. Because things usually come so easily to the brainiacs of the dog world, they can get frustrated when something isn't working out for them. If the dog is stumped on an exercise, he'll go into a canine hissy and be unable to concentrate. Stop and try again another time.

3. Have several exercises and their sequence in mind before beginning the training session. Once the bright dog understands the first command, he'll want to move right to the next challenge. Challenges are

fun. Keep 'em coming. If you don't have something new to offer him quickly, he'll lose interest.

4. Since this dog learns new commands almost immediately, it's best to stop teaching an exercise once he's performing it perfectly. If you ask him to repeat a behavior he already has down cold, his Royal Boredness will elaborate on the exercise. "How about if I add a pirouette to that jump?" the dog thinks, tired of the same old dull routine. His creativity will end up confusing both of you.

5. Training sessions themselves can be short: ten to twenty minutes, three or four times a week would be sufficient.

6. With a Caninestein, it is easy to try to progress too far, too fast. The fact that he has accomplished a command a few times does not signify that he really has it down in long-term memory. Teach one increment at a time. Practice them for a week at a time and then proceed to the next step. If you have jumped too far and he becomes confused, simply go back one or two steps and repeat them.

The Greatest Challenge

Okay, so the bright dog is tougher to train and even worse to live with. However, if you provide an interesting life for him, you can bring his destructive

behavior and his propensity to escape under control. In later chapters, we'll discuss the stimulation resulting from interesting environments, creative toys and games. However, dog experts agree that the most important aspect of an interesting life for a bright dog is making him work.

Most dogs were bred to work in concert with man. They need the chance to test and use their capabilities. Upon retiring, many very bright and successful human business executives complain that a good day at the office was always one hundred times more satisfying than a good day at the golf course. Look at the people in the universities who keep researching until they're in their eighties. Carrying out the work for which their minds are programmed provides the most satisfying life for them.

"Work" for a dog is broaching challenges and performing well. Bright dogs need goals to challenge them, rules to stick by, and rewards to strive for, just as we do. Marjorie Hudson, long-time trainer and owner of The Chosen Dog in Escondido, California, explains that on rainy days, ten minutes of obedience training can calm and satisfy a dog as much as his usual thirty-minute walk. Pet owners often have the misguided notion that it's a pain for the dog to learn commands. On the contrary, training is challenging and satisfying for a dog. In fact, many people who train their dogs often find them "asking" to work. The dog approaches them and whines. The only thing that stops the whining is working.

It's easy to see that, pretty quickly, you'll run out of the typical commands of sit, down, stay, come. Both you and the dog will end up giving

each other that deadly "thrill is gone" stare. That's where the more advanced dog sports regulated by the American Kennel Club come in. Two of these, agility and flyball, are gaining in popularity and are very good for the intelligent dog.

Agility makes obedience training more fun and complicated. Wayne Cavanaugh, vice president of communications of the American Kennel Club calls it, "the best thing that has happened to obedience training in years." In this sport, dogs must navigate ramps, balance beams (wide ones), jumps, tires, weave poles, tunnels, and many other obstacles. In tackling these tough challenges, dogs also learn sit, stay, and many other basic obedience commands, as well as how to pay attention. In a typical agility trial, a dog must tackle twenty different obstacles. The owner runs through the course with the dog, giving commands. Because the obstacles are intermingled and placed close together, the dog must think carefully to be successful.

In flyball, four dogs on a relay team run a hurdle course. When the starting whistle blows, the first dog runs over four hurdles to a flyball box. He presses the lever, which sends the ball flying into the air. He catches the ball and runs back over the hurdles. The second dog then runs the course. The series of commands involved here can get complicated, but nothing's too hard for our Caninesteins.

Flyball, agility, and even common obedience training are great sports for all dogs. Traditional obedience training does go beyond sit, down, and stay. Those who work up to the highest levels must learn many commands, work

at a distance from you, respond to hand signals, and retrieve scented objects. If you decide you want to train in any of these sports, class instructors never expect all or even most of their members to compete in trials. In fact, instructors welcome those who are simply interested in providing their dogs a more interesting life (and the owner a more peaceful one). Look at it as preschool for pups: fun activities in a structured environment with other little creatures.

If you work your dog in any sport, not only will he enjoy it, but he'll also become better behaved. However, some believe that a dog should work in the field for which he was bred. If you have a terrier, you'll notice that he focuses on anything moving in the environment. He sees a bird or a mouse and flies after it. This dog would probably love training in a sport that capitalizes on his strengths of speed and eyesight. Herding dogs, on the other hand, love to gather. Owners of border collies and Australian cattle dogs tell of their dogs herding their children, geese, even bugs! A twelve-week-old pointer pup points at a bird with no training whatsoever. Recognizing these predilections, people long ago through the American Kennel Club set up the conditions allowing their dogs' instincts to be satisfied. Below we've listed the various AKC sports and the dogs that typically participate in them. If you call the AKC at (919) 233-9767 or visit their web page (http:/www. akc.org), you can find the phone numbers of clubs in your area that organize these sports. The club (most often a breed club) secures the site and all the equipment needed; you just need to show up with your dog.

Lure Coursing: Gotta Chase!

Former racing dogs don't get much of a chance to run their potential thirty miles per hour while walking around the block with you. The Lure Coursing people have partially remedied this practical problem by setting up racing courses, which are circular or triangular tracks. Along the track's rail, a mechanism speeds along a little faster than the dogs. Out of this mechanism runs a rope with some plastic bags tied to it. The dogs must run like crazy as they try to pin that critter to the ground. Dogs most active in this sport are: Afghans, basenjis, borzois, greyhounds, Ibizan hounds, wolfhounds, Pharaoh hounds, Rhodesian Ridgebacks, salukis, Scottish deerhounds, and whippets.

Herding: Rounding Up the Fun!

In herding, dogs perform some of the tasks they would if they had a flock to supervise. Once again, a local organization has set up a farm with either ducks, sheep, or cattle to practice upon. Dogs learn to contain the flock, run it through gates, circle left, circle right, all the tasks a real working cattle or sheep dog would do. The dogs that most enjoy this sport are: Belgian Tervuren, Bouvier des Flandres, border collies, Rottweilers, Shetland sheepdogs (shelties), Australian cattle dogs, bearded collies, Belgian sheepdogs, briards, Cardigan and Pembroke Welsh corgis, collies, German shepherds, Old English sheepdogs, pulik, samoyeds, and Australian shepherds. Keep in mind that your mixed breed that has some of these breeds' blood in his veins may take to herding as if he were a purebred.

Tracking

People involved in tracking tests enjoy getting outdoors with their dogs. If you're a dog-loving hiker but not a hunter, tracking may be the sport for you. Basically, the dog is trained to follow a human scent around a course that meanders through fields and over hills. As the dog ambles along, the owner trails either with or without a twenty-foot lead. (Whether the owner uses a lead or not depends upon the reliability of the dog.) Because some tracking tests are a mile long, both you and your dog need to be in good shape. While all members of the Hound group take well to tracking, many other breeds as well as mixed breeds enjoy the sport, too.

Field and Hunting Trials: Spaniels, Pointers, and Hounds Having a Ball!

The structure and purpose of the many types of field trials depends on the breed of the dog. Depending on whether it's a spaniel, retriever, or pointer, judges focus on different aspects of the dog's performance. In most tests, a field is stocked with birds and the dogs hunt, find, flush, and retrieve the birds (hopefully without mauling them too much). In some trials, the dogs are required to retrieve a bird that has dropped into water. This sport requires an active, well-conditioned dog. Dogs that most often participate in field trials are: basset hounds, beagles, dachshunds, cocker spaniels, English springer spaniels, Brittanys, English setters, German shorthaired pointers, German wirehaired pointers, Gordon setters, Irish setters, pointers, vizslas, weimaraners, and all retrievers.

Earthdog Trials: A Terrier's Day in the Trenches

In an Earthdog trial, officials create a trench either by digging a long ditch into the ground or constructing an above-ground maze with hay bales and/or boards. The dog must navigate this complex tunnel to reach his ultimate opponent: a big, nasty rat safely protected in a cage. Participants are all terrier breeds and dachshunds who love to chase prey and don't mind getting their paws dirty.

In Conclusion...

While your Caninestein may haughtily refuse to accompany you to a Monster Truck Rally, his presence in your life brings many other benefits. How easy it is to teach him something! He seems to understand your every word. Take advantage of his dog-given abilities. Train and play with him to develop his full potential. Get him involved in activities where he can do the work he was designed for. If those sports don't wag your tail, see how he likes advanced obedience or agility training. You'll end up with a dog that's a marvel to neighbors and a joy to live with.

3

Life with the Not-So-Bright

The not-so-bright dog may be easy to contain, but getting this happy-go-lucky guy to do your bidding may land you babbling in the lap of your local shrink. However, knowing the size of your task (and it's a big one) can help you tackle it with more patience and understanding.

Signs of dimness in the dog:

1. He requires many repetitions—perhaps even thirty—before learning a new command.
2. To remember a command over a period of time, he must practice constantly.
3. If at a distance, he will not respond to a command.

4. He doesn't respond immediately and gleefully to your verbal promises of activities he enjoys, such as "go for a walk," "ride in the car," etc.
5. He'll only watch cartoons. Once you turn on PBS, he's asleep.

When you have two dogs in the house, often it's easier to determine which one got the brains. The slower dog, Pokey, tends to let Flash, the quicker dog, lead. Happy-go-lucky Pokey is content to follow his bright brother all around the house and yard looking for things to explore. When Flash goes to the vet or kennel for any period of time, Pokey sits around the house, clueless as to what to do with himself. He may even sleep all day or come and annoy you. Where the interested, curious dog gets into trouble, Pokey will probably wait for someone else to initiate the action. Even though Flash does his best to pin all the spills and lacerations on Pokey, you know better.

Before you categorize your dog as dumb, consider whether his disposition is dimming his brilliance. An overly excited or nervous dog often attacks problems without taking the time to think them through. This behavior gets in the way of careful thinking. Consider the human student who always popped up in her seat, blurting out answers throughout the class period without thinking first. She was usually way off the mark. The mind of the shy dog, too, can be eclipsed by his nervousness. In the same classroom sat a self-conscious student too timid to let her intelligence be known. It was the calm, confident student that usually impressed the class and the teacher. This bright one usually said nothing until the end of period when she leaned back in her

chair, quietly raised her hand, and pulled the whole lesson together in one sentence. Everyone was in awe. Likewise, the calm, confident dog has the best chance of utilizing his full brain power. Before you send all the college applications back, consider how you can address your dog's personality quirks so that his true potential can come through.

Why Harvard Turned Him Down

The dog who is truly dense suffers from inflexibility, which can be attributed partly to low intelligence and partly to temperament. His efforts fail most often because he tries only one solution over and over again. A new tactic never crosses his mind. He suffers from "habit fixation," the inflexibility from which the bright dog manages to escape. Further, the slower dog's observational learning skills are not very strong. Therefore, he'll have a tougher time mimicking the successful behavior of his owner or other dogs. In other words, all your cries of "Look, Pokey, like this" may fall on a hollow (but happy) head.

Another trait that slows him down is his reluctance to change a behavior that worked for him under a certain set of conditions. Once a slow dog finds something that works, he sticks too it like wet dog food, even if things change and his old behavior no longer rewards him. For example, if a slow dog has learned that a piece of food is under a towel, and then someone throws a food-scented towel on the floor but puts the food elsewhere, he will search

around and under that towel for a long time, even if no food is present. The slow dog has great difficulty inhibiting or unlearning his initial response.

Pokey's Environment

Unlike Flash, Pokey usually doesn't get into too much trouble. He tends to pass his days happily lounging around, waiting for you or another dog to provide the entertainment. His curiosity is pretty much limited to, "Is that my food coming? That's my food coming!" and "Who's petting me? Daddy's petting me. Hey! Who's that petting me? Oh yeah! Daddy's petting me." (And you always wondered why he repeatedly looks back at you while you scratch him.)

Be careful allowing him to sit around doing nothing. He does not turn a dropped dishrag into a skittering rat as the more intelligent dog does. Although he is probably content to follow the same lazy pattern day in, day out, this unstimulating lifestyle will diminish his intelligence and energy level. You have to initiate games, sometimes even prodding him to play. You also have to take him to different locations to meet other people and dogs.

Training, too, no matter how limited, goes far in jump-starting his lethargic brain cells. An owner will find that once he begins requesting behaviors from or playing good games with a torpid dog, he becomes much more alert and fun to be around. The more stimulation, the better the brain functions. The deprived brain, on the other hand, only decelerates. Consider this example involving understimulated children.

In a study carried out by the University of Indiana, researchers measured the IQ of Kentucky mountain children who had been isolated from normal educational opportunities. As researchers expected, the IQs were below average. However, once the children had taken part in normal education for a few years, the researchers tested again and found that the children's IQs had risen to average. This and many other studies prove that the brain can be changed, even enhanced. You can do the same for your dog by involving him in training, structured playing, and other activities.

We know you love your dog, but some of the dog spoiling that goes on in this country is atrocious. A dog comes up against an obstacle and the indulgent owner trips over all the furniture in a mad rush to remove it. One little whine for the dinner ham and a generous helping lands under the pup's nose. Not only does this behavior make observers nauseous, but it hinders the development of the dog's mind. The spoiled dog never reaches his intellectual potential. With no limits or expectations, he does not have to think his way through a situation. Who needs to think when anything goes! The owner who indulges her dog in this manner does him no favors.

Teaching the Not-So-Bright

Knowing that accomplishments may come slowly with Pokey will ease your frustration and keep your teeth from being ground down to little nubs. Remember, you're training him to be a helpful member of the household, but

you're also doing it for his overall well-being. Training is a lifelong process, both for Pokey and for Flash, so don't feel pressed for time.

1. Start with a routine that doesn't change too much. These dogs need regularity. They don't need challenging circumstances to conflict with the challenging things they're trying to learn. You may have to do all your work in a completely distraction-free area.
2. Break the exercise into its smallest components. Set your goals to match each small step. For a sit-stay, for example, start with getting the dog's attention. Once you've accomplished this, reward yourself and the dog.
3. Don't overwhelm him by being too animated. If he's low-energy, you will need to excite him to some extent, but don't confuse him with flailing arms and a flood of words.
4. Use hand signals as a backup to verbal commands. The clearer your instructions, the better.
5. Give one-word commands. Use the same word consistently. Owners often use, "let's go," "would you move," "hurry up," etc., when they simply mean "heel."
6. A good thing! Since Pokey doesn't get easily frustrated, you can repeat exercises many times.

In Conclusion...

While their minds may differ, both Pokey and Flash have a Love IQ that's off the charts. Your life with Pokey may be different from that of Flash's owner, but your dog brings you just as many rewards. Don't let him turn into a lethargic lump. He'll enjoy life and you much more if you put some time into developing a strong, stimulating relationship with him.

4
Jump-Starting the Puppy's Intellectual Abilities

No flash cards! For heaven's sakes burn the flash cards and forget the early foreign languages. Researchers have found that puppies who have been pushed too early rebel, often inviting the seediest dogs in the neighborhood over to help them chew up the patio furniture. No. No. It's not worth it. Despite these risks, keep in mind that there are milder activities in which you can engage your puppy that will give him the big bulging mind muscles you wish you had.

After discovering what a challenge a bright dog can be in Chapter 2, you may be more motivated to keep your pup as average as possible. Not to

worry. Brainiacs are usually born, and not too many are born at that. Over the centuries, breeders have been choosing more for docility and trainability than curiosity and intelligence. Stimulating your puppy's mind will deliver many advantages, no disadvantages. A stimulated puppy brings more joy because he:

1. develops a calm, confident, and happy personality;
2. is more entertaining—his enhanced interest in toys and new environments make him fun to watch and play with;
3. is less destructive because you've taken steps to direct his energy;
4. responds more quickly to your words and commands;
5. solves problems more quickly;
6. interacts better with other people and animals;
7. doesn't embarrass you by having to take the bar exam more than once (like that Kennedy we won't mention).

Beyond having these advantages, the owner who stimulates her pup's mind enjoys the tranquillity of knowing that her dog enjoys a more fulfilling life. A dog who is relegated to the backyard and left to live with no interaction and challenge becomes a bit brain-dead. Interested only in eating and sleeping, he fails to even make eye contact. He becomes something of a zombie, lacking emotions as well as intelligence.

But those are extreme cases. Luckily most owners are weak and pathetic.

We see our dogs looking in the door with a pitiful pout and rush to open it before the tears pour down our faces. No matter how tired we are, that puppy comes in for a cuddle or game of fetch. Too bad our nation's great leaders can't skip all the rhetoric and simply use Puppy Manipulation Tactics when negotiating trade or peace. If they could, the world would lie down for democracy.

Stimulation helps the dog have a better temperament and a happier life. For those of you looking to create Caninestein, early intervention also promises much for intellectual development. Several researchers have found that while all mammals are born with their full complement of brain cells, the right experiences and stimulation can enhance certain aspects of the brain. Dr. Marian Diamond, a University of California at Berkeley neurobiologist, found that baby rats given toys that were often changed became mentally quicker and more energetic than those who grew up with few or no toys. Upon studying their brain tissue, Diamond found that, among other benefits, the highly stimulated rats had longer, more extensive dendrites (the nerve cells across which messages travel). Further, the amount of chemicals that existed between the nerve cells (neurotransmitters) of the challenged rats had increased. These physical changes resulted in faster, more accurate decision-making, among other benefits.

Sure, dogs are not rats. (Some people are rats, but no dogs are rats.) However, as mentioned earlier, our brains are so similar it's not outrageous to assume that what's good for one mammal is good for all. In fact, based on

her own research and the similar research of others, Dr. Diamond set up a special preschool for disadvantaged children that provides the enrichment opportunities these students may not otherwise receive. The ultimate goal is to make sure these children do not remain behind their peers. By jump-starting their students' minds with specialized activities, Diamond and her colleagues have achieved remarkable results.

Early stimulation has other advantages. Studies show that infant rats, kittens, and dogs who were given socialization, enrichment, and early handling have these similarities:

1. greater resistance to physical and emotional stress and diseases;
2. enhanced learning abilities because of emotional stability;
3. an outgoing personality that will help lead him into learning situations;
4. blatant rejection of Barney and Thomas the Tank Engine.

Clearly, research proves that efforts to increase the brain's abilities do pay off.

Despite the fact that we want the best for our pups, today's realities make it hard to give him the stimulation he needs. With both Mom and Dad at work and the kids at school all day, the pup spends a lot of time alone. Nonetheless, you can provide an enriched environment that will nourish his mind.

Puppy's Environment

So you've brought your puppy home and, hopefully, you've taken a few days off work to help him adjust to his new sur-roundings. Now—where to keep him? Some books suggest that if can you come home at noon, it's best to keep the puppy in a crate in the hours in between. That

plan may work well for house-training, but it does not maximize puppy's brain power. The limited surroundings prevent him from doing much other than sleeping. He has no chance to explore and play while you're gone. The more adventures he can get into, the more his brain labors to grow those squirrelly dendrites.

A better plan is to keep him in a larger area, preferably the kitchen. You can also use a large wire exercise pen placed in the kitchen or any appropri-ate area. While the regular exercise pen may only provide about fifteen square feet, you can hook two together to create a larger area. With active puppies, you may need to brace the corners so the puppies don't knock the whole thing over. A scrap piece of linoleum serves well as a floor under the pen.

At first, cover the entire area with papers. Place his bed in one corner, his food in another. He won't want to eliminate in either area, and therefore

he'll do his business in the area furthest from these points. Day by day remove some papers until he's eliminating in one corner.

If you work at home and plan to keep the pup with you, watch him closely as he wakes and after he eats. Always take him outside to your preferred elimination areas at those times. You may also want to keep a leash on him that you tuck under your leg as you work at your desk. Connected to you, he cannot wander too far to eliminate in a corner. He'll also feel more secure with a direct connection to you. When you feel confident that he doesn't need to eliminate, let him off the leash to explore the room.

To develop a first-class mind, a pup needs more in his living quarters than newspapers.

1. Fill the room with toys (make sure they're large enough that he can't swallow them). Ten different toys are not too many and more would be even better. Catalogs such as R. C. Steele (1-800-872-3773), Doctors Foster & Smith (1-800-826-7206), Omaha Vaccine Company (1-800-367-4444), and others carry toys at costs much lower than those in the pet supply stores and grocery stores. Through the catalogs, you can even get three high-quality toys in a batch for around seven dollars. If you have a friend with a puppy or dog, arrange it so that the nondestroyed but abandoned toys are kept and traded.

   Caution: some puppies make it their life's work to chew the squeaker out of vinyl and latex toys. If you have a puppy like this, do not leave

him alone with any toys that contain squeakers. A swallowed squeaker lodged in the pup's digestive system requires surgical removal.

2. Rotate groups of toys. Keep the same seven or so toys in the pup's environment for two weeks. Pick them up, wash them, and put them away. Bring out seven other toys for the dog and repeat the process. It would be great if you could have four different groups of toys. Novelty! Novelty! Novelty!

3. Make sure the toys are of all varieties. Buy a few each of latex, vinyl, soft stuffed animals, balls, ropes, Frisbee flying disks, bones, etc. The differing textures, noises, and shapes will keep the puppy busy investigating.

4. Yes, puppies do get bored with their toys and you may run through quite a few. Two weeks may be all the time a pup plays with a toy. To make sure that the brain is getting all it should, be ready with new toys! The rats that had the thickest cortexes and most neurotransmitters were those whose toys were changed often. Remember, toys to a puppy don't have to be bought in a store. Old socks knotted together, washed plastic milk jugs, cardboard boxes, old rags, bicycle-tire inner tubes with the valve cut out, and many other household items can look just as fun to a pup as something that cost $4.95 at PetCo.

5. Put a sturdy box or tunnel in his living area. Climbing on and through objects will give him a new perspective and teach him new

skills. A small ramp with a flat area on top (no higher than one foot) would be ideal.

6. Make sure to have a nice crate for him to retire to. Pups feel very secure in their crates, the modern day equivalent of the wild dog's cave. The more emotionally secure a dog feels, the more likely he is to explore and accept challenges. *Caution: keep crates and tunnels away from gates or sides of a pen so the pup cannot jump out.*

7. Leave a radio playing in his living area. Not only will the human voices be comforting, but they'll get your puppy accustomed to different words and tones of voice. When you speak to him later, he'll have a stronger frame of reference.

8. Once you're home, allow the dog to explore other areas of the house (you may want to have a leash on him while he does this in case he begins to squat to eliminate). Dogs often learn by accident. He'll lean against a door and it will open. He'll find an obstacle and learn to climb under or around it. Your puppy needs to have as much exposure as possible to these learning opportunities.

9. Consider keeping four or five toys away from the dog during the day. When you come home, bring out those four or five and play with him with those. Once the evening is over, put them away. These toys will have added value because they are not available all the time. More interested, the puppy will explore them enthusiastically.

A planned stimulating environment will provide plenty of challenges for your dog's developing brain. These modifications are not too tough to pull off and they'll make a huge difference not only in the puppy's daily life, but also in his personality as an adult dog. Many dogs become big lumps. To enhance activity and inquisitiveness in your dog, start by making his daily environment exciting.

Teaching During the Different Stages of the Pup's Life

Think of all the goofy stages a child goes through from birth to eighteen years of age. During some years, parents must be there playing backup for the child's every tiny catastrophe. Later, we can't get closer than five feet before they shrink away from us as if our teeth were dropping out of our heads from rot. Children go through several crucial stages where aspects of their adult personality form. Dogs, too, pass through stages, but they're much more efficient about it. They get it done all in about a year and a half. Each stage in a dog's first months requires special consideration.

For those of you lucky enough to be involved in the puppy's birth and early weeks, there are things you can do to awaken his mental processes and strengthen his personality at the same time. Charles Pfaffenberger, who helped develop the Guide Dogs for the Blind program in the early thirties, conducted a research study to determine how to improve the percentage of

competent dogs. Dismayed at how many dogs were unfit to be guide dogs even after lots of training, he wanted to be able to control some of the factors that contribute to personality. He found that the puppy's experience with his mother had a great effect on his adult temperament. A good mother dog produces confident puppies. Confident puppies are brave enough to explore their environment. They also face obstacles and try to solve the problems rather than run from them. These self-satisfied pups usually had a loving but authoritative mother. She dotes on them, but when they cross her boundaries, *splat*! She squashes them flat with a big paw. A mother dog who overpunishes creates pups too fearful to take on the challenges that stimulate their minds. A mother dog who underpunishes, on the other hand, turns out puppies that are totally out of control. No parental discipline can produce a canine juvenile delinquent! Their problem-solving abilities may be impaired because they simply fly at an obstacle rather than undertaking it in a rational and eventually successful way.

If you plan to buy a puppy from a breeder, try to see the mother and the rest of the littermates at home. As you evaluate a pup (or a spouse for that matter), keep one eye on the mother. If she seems very aggressive, be careful. Remember, too, since you're there evaluating the puppy, he's probably six weeks old or so. At this point, the mother is trying to wean her batch of constantly starving sucklers and rightfully so. She may be running from them and growling to some extent. Ask the breeder what the mother was like, and try to pet her yourself to see if she's basically friendly. The majority

of mother dogs do a bang-up job. Those errant few, however, can ruin a pup's personality.

Make sure to ask when the puppies were removed from the mother. Some breeders remove the mother from her litter as early as three to four weeks. At that time, they prevent the pups from interacting with any adult dogs. These puppies do not learn proper canine social skills. Early separation from the mother can also affect their interaction with people.

The Early Weeks

Brand new puppies in the house are hard to resist. The good news: you no longer have to stand by the whelping nest melting and whimpering because you can't touch these furry little fatties. Researchers have discovered that carefully stroking the tiny pup aids brain development.

There is barely any EEG activity from the period of birth to two weeks; the brain is still in the process of forming itself. It's getting some stimuli from the mother and littermates. If you throw very mild stress in the equation, you'll help the brain grow even more.

Dr. Michael Fox stimulated pups with stroking, clicks, flashes of light, and gentle balance exercises from the period of birth to two weeks. As adults, these dogs had larger adrenal glands than those that hadn't been stimulated. Further, they solved the problems they were faced with not only more quickly, but more calmly. On problem-solving tests, the stimulated

dogs were much more successful than their unstimulated counterparts. Giving a brand new pup a mild dose of the stresses he'll encounter later in life enables him to meet those challenges with more intelligence and confidence. In his book *Superdog: Raising the Perfect Canine Companion,* Fox suggests that during the neonatal period, owners should pick the puppy up and pet it for a few minutes every day. While Fox also suggests that owners place the pup on a cold surface from time to time, we prefer putting our pups on varied surfaces: newspapers, towels, carpets, etc.

Learning in the Transitional Period: 2–4 Weeks

At about two weeks, your grunting, whimpering balls of cuteness begin to open their eyes. At three weeks, EEGs show that the pup's brain is being stimulated by the sights and sounds of the world around him. The pup's eyes begin to develop at two weeks, and by twenty-eight days his sight is very close to that of an adult. Finally capable of walking a bit, he begins to wander from the nest. Hearing develops at the same time.

In a study carried out at Adelphi University, Adler and Adler discovered that pups are capable of observational learning soon after their eyes have become functional. That means that they can learn how to do things by watching others. Since they are much more comfortable with littermates at this point, it's best to allow pups to learn from each other. Your tutelage will be much appreciated *later*. At this point, the pup needs to be with mother

and littermates to learn dog rules and behavior. During this transitional stage:

1. continue to gently stroke the pups once a day;
2. if you have a more sluggish pup, try to pair him with an active, curious pup that explores a lot;
3. give the explorers of the litter things to explore: boxes, toys, rags;
4. create lumps in the puppy pen by putting pieces of toweling or crumpled newspapers under the main floor covering;
5. since they're barely walking, stimulation should be mild: don't expect them to wander too far from the nest;
6. begin to tease the pup gently by moving toys in front of him and allowing him to paw at them. Make sure to allow him to be successful. Don't tease too much.

The Socialization Period: 4–12 Weeks

Dog experts concur: this is the most crucial stage of the pup's development. It's at this time that dogs form their relationships with other mammals, human and canine. From this point until sixteen weeks, having stable relationships with both is crucial.

From four to six weeks, the pup's littermates and mother should be its closest pals. By seven weeks, the pup should be playing and interacting regu-

larly with people. Pfaffenberger found that the best time to introduce a puppy to its life work and those who will be its pack members (new owner and family members) was six weeks. Between six and eight weeks, the pup's desire to investigate and make contact overcomes its fear. While at this time the pup seems very brave, shortly he'll become something of a coward. Between eight and ten weeks, the puppy passes through a "fear period." It's important at this time to avoid frightening situations. If the dog is afraid of something, don't force him to go near it. If he doesn't want to participate in an activity, don't make him.

During the socialization period, these activities will help the dog grow familiar with human language, the process of learning, and the fine art of problem solving. During the socialization period:

1. Allow him to put his face directly into something he's exploring (unless it's a guest's lap). Dogs have sensory hairs called "vibrissae" on their muzzles, below their jaws, and above their eyes. Not only can dogs determine the shape and texture of objects with these vibrissae, but they can also judge airflow. By burying their

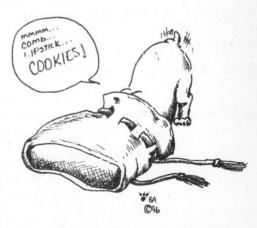

faces in whatever they're exploring, they're adding to their storehouse of knowledge. A nose in your purse is not a grab for a lipstick snack as much as a noble expedition.

2. As you start to do things with your dog, name them. Saying "ride in the car," "go for a walk," and "eat dinner" as you begin each activity will help the dog associate an activity with your words. Don't make the mistake of thinking that all he'll ever learn is "sit," "down," and "no."

3. To all you overprotective parents: don't jump in and solve all his problems for him. If he gets tangled in something, give him a chance to get himself out. If a toy is stuck under a bureau and he's whimpering, let him try a few solutions. Don't rush in and wipe out all obstacles. Allow him to explore and try different strategies to deal with the situation. Of course, if the situation is hopeless, step in like a good parent and save the day.

4. Start training with very minor commands. "Sit" is a simple one. Teaching your puppy to stand still now can do him some good. Not only will he be easier to groom and bathe, but he'll learn self-control—standing in one place without moving his feet can be tough for the wiggly pup. It's rather like the kindergartner learning the important lessons of staying still and attentive.

5. Allow him to climb over you.

6. Allow him to paw at objects and change their position. He's discovering an object's potential.

7. Watch the litter for shy puppies. These guys will have a tougher time throughout life. You can turn it around early. Play with the shy fellow. Tug-of-war games that encourage a little aggression serve well, but remember to always end the game when you want to. Massage and groom. These activities will help the pup trust you and his own abilities to deal with challenges. Challenges lead to learning opportunities.

8. After his shots inoculate him against common diseases, start taking him places in the car. Take him to parks, malls, friends' homes—any different environment. Once there, allow him to sniff and explore. Researchers have found that you can maximize inherited intelligence by exposing your pup to a wide variety of experiences and situations during this stage. Two products that make toting the puppy around easier are The Dog-Gone Device and the Pac a Pet, both modified from carriers designed for children. The Dog-Gone Device is a backpack that holds a dog up to twenty pounds. The dog's head clears the pack, but a collar keeps him stationary. For more information call (800) 367-7303. Similar to the Snugli baby carrier, the Pac a Pet holds puppies and small dogs on the owner's chest. Their number is (208) 853-4845. Similar carriers are also available in the pet supply catalogs.

These activities help him become a better problem-solver as an adult:

1. Put him in his crate and then unlock it, but leave the door in the shut position. Call him and see if he can push open the gate and come to you.

2. While playing with him, hide his toy under your hand, a pillow, or towel. Allow him to search for it for a while, but also allow him to be successful. Give him hints by lifting the corner of the barrier up so he can see the toy. This exercise is probably more effective after the pup is eight weeks old.

3. Put him at the bottom of two stairs and encourage him to climb them. You'll probably have to sit up the stairs from him and encourage him to come to you.

4. Put a favorite toy just inside the door of the closet so he can see it. Allow him to fight with the door a bit but give him some help if it looks like it's going to overwhelm him.

5. Put him on the other side of a door that's open a bit so he can see you. Call him.

6. Pile up a bunch of old pillows. Put him on one side, go to the other side and sit down. Call him to you. Allow him to crawl over and navigate the pillows to get to Mommy/Daddy. Don't be surprised if he can't resist the soft cushions, which call to him to nap with every step.

7. Put him in one room and go to an area you don't usually occupy. Call him and let him find you.

The Juvenile Period: 4–6 Months

An extension of the socialization period, the juvenile period lasts a few months before adolescence sets in. During this period, puppies should continue their course of socialization. Meeting other dogs and people both at home and at new places keeps their minds occupied. As we mentioned earlier, mental stimulation tires a dog as quickly as physical stimulation. Since your pup is probably a hypermaniac at this point, this fact is useful. It is now that you should get him spayed or neutered. Continue training and seriously consider entering a puppy class. Many puppy classes offer "play time" where the dogs run around together before formal training starts.

The Angst of Adolescence

The onset of psoriasis— Oh, excuse us, we meant to write "Adolescence." Yes, the onset of adolescence brings with it instances of assertion, independence, even aggression. A loving, goofy puppy in the morning, he may deteriorate into a sullen, partially deaf slug by the afternoon. He doesn't respond to the commands you know he knows. He begins urinating on your Ming vases. He asks for his own telephone and to have his room painted black. As wise trainers say, "this too shall pass." However, many trainers pick up the phone only to hear, "this too is not passing!"

Relax. Stand your ground. Accept that you will be exerting more energy for the next nine to twelve months. Get him to participate in all of the activities listed above. Your greater struggle will be getting his attention and com-

pliance. When the dog fails to sit, put him in a sit (if you're sure he won't bite you). When the dog fails to down, put him down. At this point, you may have to resort to some gentle dominance behaviors. While you may not seem to be getting anywhere, you are. Your fortitude now reaps dividends in later years. You'll be surprised when one day, the dog just starts complacently following each of your commands as if he never was a stubborn pain in the butt and always accepted your authority. However, if you don't lay down the law now, you could have a dog who acts adolescently well into his senior years. Twelve years of adolescence? Most prefer to be tough now. Pay close attention to the following areas.

1. Playing: make sure you choose which toys to play with and how long the game is going to last. If the dog always ends the game, he begins to feel he's the boss.
2. Sleeping: can you move your dog if he is sleeping? If he growls when you try to move him from his favorite spot, he feels he can intimidate you. A submissive dog in a pack *never* growls at the leader dog. You are the leader. Do not permit him to growl or snap at you. Get professional help from a trainer if there's any indication he may bite.
3. Grooming: does your dog accept your grooming and petting, even toenail cutting? During the day, when the dog is resting or involved in something, begin grooming him. The leader dog grooms subordinate dogs any time he feels like it.

4. Eating: don't give in to begging. You must decide when and where the dog eats. The dog should not eat with you. Ideally, he should eat his meal after you've finished yours.

By four months, your dog's physical growth is two-thirds complete. Now that he is big enough, he can learn from observing you.

1. If he is reluctant to go through his doggie door, crawl through it yourself (or send one of your children). If you're training in agility and want him to leap over obstacles or stand on low tables, run through these activities yourself. *Caution: pups under fifteen months old should never jump higher than half the length of their foreleg.*
2. Begin playing some of the more complicated games listed in Chapter 6.

In Conclusion...

While it's probably the most fun, the puppy stage is also the most difficult for you as an owner. You're getting used to your new responsibilities and the bizarre inner life of a dog. To make sure your dog will become very interesting to you and interested in his life, lead him into the activities that will bring his mind to its full potential. You've got at least ten years together: you might as well lay a good foundation while he's too short and squeaky to object.

5

Hey There Lonely Girl: Dogs Educating and Entertaining Themselves While Mom and Dad Are At Work

When you come home from work, does your dog plaster you with paws and slobber? You have to remind him that, yes, you really were there that very morning; no, you haven't been gone for months. He isn't easily convinced.

Are we just giving our dogs human characteristics when we think they feel lonely? No. Many dogs, especially the only-dog, feel bored and frustrated

when left alone for long periods of time. Making some changes in his daily environment can alleviate some of these negatives.

To consider what is appropriate for a dog if he had his druthers, we can look at one of the progenitors of dogs: wolves. Wolves spend the day hunting, sleeping, grooming each other, and playing. To find enough food, they run an average of thirty miles a day. Left only to their own wits to survive, they are significantly challenged physically and mentally.

Echoes of this unfettered lifestyle still haunt domestic dogs today. Granted, with shelter and food delivered to them in a thousand different brands, our pets have it much easier. Some party poopers complain that domestic dogs languish in "arrested adolescence" with all their needs met through no effort of their own. While our dogs are spoiled in a sense, they are also being deprived of the challenges that make their ancestors so frighteningly bright. Consider the retiree whose health declines dramatically after he stops working, or the institutionalized who seem to become the walking dead. Without daily challenge, the ability to solve problems diminishes. Without adequate socialization, behavior and disposition deteriorates. It's easy to see how the dog who's left alone for the majority of his life devolves from *canis domesticus* to *lumpis big fattus*.

In an environment where the dog is understimulated and isolated, several problems can occur. Bored dogs destroy couches, shoes, handbags, dining room tables, you name it. Once the vandalism gets dull, the dog sleeps the day—and his life—away. In their search for something to do, some dogs

even lick their foreleg excessively, creating an open sore that eventually requires medical attention.

I'm Going to Disneyland!—Creating an Intriguing Environment for Your Dog

As you move pieces of paper from one pile to another at work, does this thought cross your mind: "I wonder what Little Pumpkin's doing right now . . ." You grimace as the image arises: your dog lying flat, mouth half open, snoring. Flies land on his tongue and teeth as he can't even rouse enough consciousness to snap them away. What if his environment offered more? It's not difficult to provide incentives for him to explore and observe, even if you're not actually on the scene.

Dogs who spend their days both inside and outside can benefit from the goodie bag. San Diego Trainer Carol Schatz recommends this little trick. Pack a brown paper lunch bag with small toys, chews, and treats, and then close it tightly. When you're ready to leave for the day, use the goodie bag to lead the dog to the area where he'll be staying. His first challenge will be to get the bag open to win the prize. After he shuffles through and finds all the treats, the goodie bag will keep him busy for a while as he goes from toys to treats to chews. Because it contains such a variety of enticements, the goodie bag serves as something of a play schedule. The dog goes from chewing to eating to playing. Another benefit is that in giving it to the dog when you're

about to leave, your departure becomes less terrible. While the departure moment deprives him of you, the goodie bag he gets brings fun and food. Schatz has seen dogs who immediately rip the bag open and others who gently undo it and carefully remove the contents one item at a time.

Whether your dog spends the day inside or outside, there are many motivating modifications you can make. If your dog stays inside all day, consider these improvements:

1. The larger the space he has to explore, the better. Allow him access to as many rooms as possible.

2. Find an area where you can give him access to a window. Dogs like to see what's going on. The best window is the one from which he can see the most action. Provide a sturdy box or chair for him to stand on so he can be comfortable observing a day in the neighborhood. If the dog stays on your enclosed porch, consider replacing part of the solid wall with a strong lattice. A small portion will do. Not only can your dog check out the action, but passing animals may approach him to say hello. Owners are surprised to find that a window to the world does not necessarily mean the dog will bark more. Dogs bark at strange noises. If they're able see the source of that noise, they often stop barking.

3. Hide treats and bones around the dog's living area. At first, put him in a sit-stay or have someone restrain him as you go about hiding the

treats. He'll remember where a couple of them are, but will have to hunt for the rest. Once he realizes that you are planting these objects daily, put him out of the room while you do your hiding. The search for them will become fun and stimulating. Change their location. Skip a day.

4. Put on a radio or television. Dogs are comforted and stimulated by human voices. If you don't want either running for too long, hook them up to appliance timers which you can find easily in a home supply store. Set the timer to turn the television or radio on at noon and off at two o'clock. When he does want it to be quiet for sleeping, he doesn't have to hear noise all day long. *Caution: make sure the radio and all cords are out of his reach.*

If your dog spends his days in a yard, these strategies can help:

1. Hang objects from the trees or any structure overhanging your yard. A dog can entertain himself by batting around a tire, board, plastic pipe, or bone.

2. If his doghouse has a roof, consider affixing a ramp to it so that the dog can reach the top and relax there. If your dog house doesn't have a flat roof, use your carrying crate. Putting a few screw or nail holes into that sturdy plastic isn't going to hurt it. Build a table if you must. Dogs enjoy sitting up high, which is probably a throwback to the wolves and wild dogs that use lookout mounds to survey the horizon. In one study, researchers found that when they put a higher area into a laboratory environment, dogs spent 54 percent of their time on top of the raised structure. (Make sure none of your ramps or agility equipment is high enough or close enough to the fence to enable the dog to escape from your yard.)

3. Do you have a dog who loves to take the stuffing out of his bed? You've seen how focused and determined he is on emptying every piece of fiberfill from the nylon sack. It's a challenge! To divert that energy, find a wooden crate with an opening that measures about four or five inches square. Affix it to something sturdy. Place a couple of aromatic treats in it and then stuff it with old rags. The dog will have to spend some time pulling all of those rags out. For some dogs,

the treat isn't even necessary! The sense of accomplishment at empty-ing the crate does enough for him. You can modify this idea by using a sturdy nylon bag.

4. Since dogs are very active, we need strategies that encourage them to expend energy. Put agility equipment in the yard. Ramps, tunnels, and jumps give the dog something to do other than pace. If you train the dog in agility, he will probably use the equipment even more. You can get a tunnel for a reasonable price at any children's store like Toys "Я" Us. For a jump, find four bricks and a 2" x 10" board. Pinion the board with the bricks. A stabilized refrigerator box makes a decent tunnel.

THE CANINE ATHLETE
IN HEAVY TRAINING

5. Like the inside dog, the dog who stays in the yard will have a great time finding the treats and bones that you hide throughout his living area.

Creative Toy Alternatives

As with puppies, having a lot of toys around for adult dogs keeps them playing and exploring. New toys stimulate the growth of neural patterns in the brain. What is this toy? the dog asks himself. What can it do? What happens when I crush it and stomp it and chew it all up? Sadly, these questions are answered pretty quickly. Yes, dogs grow bored with new toys as quickly as children do. Luckily, dogs also forget stuff.

To avoid the expensive habit of buying new toys to stimulate, group your toy collection into several separate sets with five or six toys in each set. When the dog starts ignoring one set, clean it, put it away, and bring out another. Constant rotation makes toys seem new.

Another way to turn toys into a mental workout is to enhance them with food. Forcing the dog to work for a snack will exercise his mind. Remember, he's used to having dinner put in front of him—no thought power required there. With several of the toys below, he's forced to paw, rip, roll, and pounce to win his snack. Wolves must work hard to bring down a caribou. Because of these challenges, wolves' brains are 16 percent larger than those of our domesticated dogs. Despite this minor difference, our dogs have a lot more

brain capacity than they are using. Making a snack tough to get doesn't constitute teasing our dogs. Rather, it intrigues and excites them. Consider adding these food-enhanced toys to your dog's environment:

1. The heavy rubber Kong toys that have a hollow center are prime for stuffing. Jam your dog's favorite treats into the center, making sure that—while a few can come out—the best and biggest is wedged up there permanently.

2. Real sterilized beef marrow bones stuffed with cheese can keep a dog licking for hours.

3. Drill Nylabones with small holes and fill the holes with Cheez Whiz.

4. Wrap flavored, sterilized marrow bones or flavored rawhide chews in newspaper and masking tape. Did you envision a big mess waiting for you when you get home? You're right! But what's a little sweeping when it comes to your dog's intellectual workout?

5. The Buster Cube is an ingenious toy that keeps dogs going for a while. It's a six-inch plastic square with a small opening on one side. You pour small pellets of dry food through this opening. The inside is divided into several compartments that prevent the pellets from pouring out all at once. The dog must roll the Cube around with his paws and nose to release the food one piece at a time. This toy puts a bit of the challenge back into retrieving food. It comes complete with

a pamphlet discussing the importance of stimulating the dog's mind. You can find it in the pet supply catalogs or by asking your local pet store to order it.

6. One study found that among rawhide chews, plastic piping, and Gumabone chews, the chews most munched upon were Gumabone.

7. A cardboard box with a treat inside gives the dog two fun challenges. Big cardboard boxes are fun to destroy. And when all the destruction is finished, there's a crispy treat inside! What more could a dog want? Besides, throwing a cardboard box with a treat inside to the dog just as you're leaving for work distracts him from this disappointing part of his day.

Beyond the mental stimulation dogs receive from working for their treats, these absorbing challenges can even ease behavior problems. Focused on appropriate objects, they don't have the time to consider destroying your rubber band collection. If a food-enhanced chew seems too basic for you, consider the gambler who sits in front of a slot machine for hours. Occasional small rewards (a few coins) keep the player interested in the elusive jackpot. Similarly, toys that produce small rewards during chewing or pawing but keep the final reward difficult to obtain provide the dog with the same thrill. With a few food-enhanced toys lying around, you can bet your dog will give up a bit of his nap time to tackle them.

A Friend of His Own

Isn't it time you started licking the insides of your dog's ears? How about rolling around on the floor biting his face while he bites yours? If you're not participating in these activities now, we think you should begin right away. Come on: what's a little dog fur between the teeth? Either that or get your dog another dog or cat to play with, especially if he spends ten hours of the day alone.

Giving your dog a same-species companion or even a cat to play with has many benefits. Dr. Michael Fox has found that dogs who live with another dog not only tend to be healthier but they more effectively resist diseases that pass through their communities.

Two dogs together can carry out some of the activities that go on in a pack. The dogs spend more time playing (as only dogs can play), grooming, and exploring. With more play, physique improves. A dog wrestling match enhances problem-solving abilities. In their shot at mock-triumph, they are forced to find ways to vanquish each other. They push each other to the ground, wrestle over toys, and try to outrun each other. For wild canids, play is a dress rehearsal for the more serious activities in life. Adult wolves don't play. Their

offspring play in order to learn how to fight and capture prey. Since nothing so serious as actual self-sufficiency will ever come our dogs' way, dog play provides one of the few challenges available to them.

Beyond the thrill that play provides, two dogs together tend to explore more. One alerts the other to the presence of treacherous trespassers like big spiders. Owners of two dogs often report seeing their dogs watching a spider and hearing them whisper, "You get it." "No you get it." "You get it. I got the last one." "You have the tissue. You get it. We'll throw it down the toilet and watch it spin." Together, they double-team these intruders. When one discovers something interesting, the other is not far behind.

Ah, but two dogs are twice as much work! Not necessarily. First and foremost, with another dog pal, you are no longer required to meet 100 percent of your dog's needs for love, entertainment, and security. The dog now has another to sleep with, wrestle with, and groom. You can also learn to walk two dogs very easily, especially if they are small ones. When coauthor Suzanne Delzio walks her two dogs, people walking one dog often approach her and say sadly, "I know my dog would love to have a dog friend." Owners instinctively know that their dogs long for a pal. The few additional tasks are well worth the joy a second pet brings to all the household mammals.

Despite the benefits most dogs receive from having a same species companion, there are those mutts who really and truly want to be an only dog. Rescued dogs and those found at the pound may bar the door to a second dog. Why? These guys have often been abused or at least seriously neglected.

Once they latch on to a human that loves them, they aren't gonna share, no way, no how. You can easily determine whether your dog wants you all to himself by bringing in a second dog for a trial period. Always be present when the two dogs are together. If after a week the first dog still snaps and growls at the second, it's probably best that you keep your first dog as the sole recipient of your affection.

Those thinking of getting a second dog should take some precautions.

1. Make sure that you can take the second dog for a trial period. You want to make sure the two dogs get along. Be careful for the first month. Try to be present at all times when they are together. Unless it's clear that it's love at first sight, keep them in separate areas when you can't be with them.
2. If the second dog is of the opposite sex, the two will generally get along better.
3. Introduce the second dog to the first on neutral ground outside the home so your first dog does not become territorial. After the introduction on neutral territory, most dogs are happy to invite another into their home.
4. If your second dog is a puppy, have a separate pen or place for the puppy for the first two months when you are not home. Puppies can annoy an adult dog to the snapping point. They also cannot handle as much space as your adult dog.

5. If your first dog is a puppy, it's best to allow him to grow to twelve or eighteen months before you bring in a second pet. Your pup needs that time to bond to you. Two puppies raised together may be more interested in each other than in you. Secondly, their individual personalities will have a better chance to develop fully if they are not competing with a same age companion.

6. If you decide a cat is your better option, it's best to get a kitten so that it can grow up with the dog. An adult cat may be frightened of a well-meaning but clumsy dog.

If you'd like to have a second dog that's a pedigree, consider contacting the rescue organizations affiliated with local breed clubs. When an owner of a particular breed can no longer keep their dog, they call the breed rescue club who finds a member to foster it until another owner can be found. City-run shelters also contact the rescue organizations to inform them of when a dog of that breed has come in. To find a breed rescue club in your area, call the American Kennel Club at (212) 696-8231 or visit their web site at http://www.akc.org.

The Day Care Option

For some owners there are no answers other than—you guessed it—private school. Their dogs just aren't getting enough. Perhaps the most impressive

private school for dogs is the Doggy Daycare Center operated by the San Francisco chapter of the S.P.C.A. Recognizing the angst of working dog-moms and -dads, they opened the mother of all day care facilities. For $25 a day, your dog can play in a wading pool, work out on exercise equipment, request intermittent walks, and even watch his favorite shows on a big-screen TV. The dogs are with people all day (unless they want to retire to their individual "apartments" for a nap). A large yard surrounding the complex provides plenty of room for the dogs to romp. Once they come in, they deposit their belongings in lockers, meet their playmates, and then begin a set schedule of play and training, which will leave them spent by the end of the day. When the owner arrives after a long day of work, he and the dog have a similar energy level. They can both go home and crash in front of the television.

But you don't have to go all the way to San Francisco to take advantage of the benefits there. Local kennels are becoming more willing to take day care babies. They're finding that the demand is great (translation: you won't be the only weirdo putting your dog in day care). Of course these are not as luxurious as San Francisco's, but they still serve a purpose. Dr. Patrick Melese, a San Diego veterinarian and behaviorist, claims that the stimulation from the car rides to the kennel and back, as well the opportunity to see a new environment, people, and dogs enrich your pet's life.

When considering the option of day care, one should be as cautious as when choosing day care for a child. Follow these guidelines:

1. Make sure the kennel requires current vaccination records from all boarders.
2. Check out the kennel's safety strategies. If all dogs play together, they should be neutered. Two unneutered males can fight viciously, especially if a female in season saunters in. Make sure someone monitors the dogs the entire time they are together.
3. Find out the kennel's emergency plan in case of illness or accident.
4. Survey where the dogs will be staying. The elimination area must be separate from the play area.
5. Make sure the toys are safe and large enough so they cannot be swallowed.

In Conclusion...

Filling your dog's days with more excitement and challenge can do wonders for his mind, mood, and energy level. By making these few adjustments, you won't have to cringe as much as you leave for work. A study conducted by the Companion Animal Research Group in England concluded, "physical [environment] enrichment has been shown to be particularly valuable as it allows dogs to exercise greater choice in behavior throughout the day." A dog who has spent the day playing, exploring, and observing neighborhood events greets you with much less frenetic need. You, too, feel more satisfied that you're doing all you can to give your dog a fulfilling life.

6
Games Brainiacs Play

How old were you when you began to look upon Candyland with disdain? And checkers? A little baby game for second-graders, you told your mother. How do you think your dog is feeling about simple fetch at this point? And you thought he was throwing up because he had eaten some grass…It's time to bring him up to the world of advanced toys and games.

Since dogs are somewhat clumsy with Nintendo, we have to be creative in finding stimulating games we can play with them. Luckily, a dog's enthusiasm and patience make him a great play partner. Beside the description of each game is a marker indicating which aspect of intelligence the game inspires. While all games are designed for canine and human delight, each emphasizes one of the four components of intelligence we've explored:

 problem-solving

 memory

 language comprehension

 learning ability

While playing, be careful not to overplay. Some dogs will happily play themselves into heatstroke or respiratory failure. Stop if his breathing becomes labored or his eyes glazed. Vomiting phlegm or lack of bright pink tongue color are also signs of distress. Be particularly careful with the brachycephalic breeds (flat-faced bulldogs, Pekingese, etc.) who don't handle heat as well as their long-nosed counterparts.

Games

Remember, novelty was the key to a brain that constantly develops more connections, flexibility, insight, and memory. Most owners simply resort to a few throws of the tennis ball for their dogs. The novelty in that exercise wore off after about three sessions of that game. By learning a few new games, you can keep your dog's mind growing.

To be beneficial to the dog's brain development, these games must have rules that you stick to. With enticing rewards, your dog will quickly catch on to all of them. Sometimes the dog will participate in the game because it's fun in itself. For others, the food makes it fun. Your squeals of delight and excited petting also reward the dog. Feel free to laugh and move around like you're having fun. Remember, happy dogs are wiggle worms. You should show your enthusiasm by doing the same. If your dog can't perform a solid sit-stay, you may need to have another person helping you, holding the dog from time to time.

To increase your dog's ability to comprehend language, give each game a simple name that you like. As you're about to play, get his attention and tell him the name of the game. The dog learns to connect one or two words with an activity (keep the number of words to a minimum). When you start training him, he'll be better able to connect your words with the activity you're looking for. He'll also be more familiar with what your tone of voice indicates.

The baseball game below comes from Camp Winnaribbun, a retreat that caters to dogs in Lake Tahoe, Nevada.

Two-Person, Two-Dog Baseball

This game (often played with an adult and child) makes baseball a little easier on the humans, and a lot more fun for the dogs. The dogs will be expected to get the balls and bring them back to the pitcher. One dog stands

behind the pitcher, another behind the batter. The pitcher throws the ball. If the batter misses, the catcher dog retrieves the ball and brings it to the pitcher. If the ball is hit, the outfielder dog retrieves the ball and brings it to the pitcher. While it may sound complicated, this game contains only the elements of fetch, stay, and drop it. At first, it may need to be taught with others restraining one dog, the catcher dog for instance, while the outfielder dog does his job and vice versa.

Owner and Dog Hide and Seek

Holding small pieces of treats, call your dog to you. When he comes, say "good dog." Put several of the treats on the ground so that the dog will be occupied while you walk about ten feet from him. Once you see he's almost finished with the treats, call him, "Dog, come!" When he reaches you, put more treats down and move ten feet in another direction, staying in plain sight of him. Again, he'll be occupied while you move away. Once the dog

gets this part of the game down, add another dimension. Put the treats down and move away from your dog—but hide. At first, just go around the corner, but as his skill level increases you can become very inventive. Call the dog and allow him to look for you. Once he finds you, say "good dog" and put more treats on the ground. Hide again. Once he catches on to finding you while you hide, stop calling him. He'll have to hunt for you in the places he knows you hide. When he finds you, reward him again with treats. This game works well with cat food or any small bits of food that will keep the dog occupied but not overfed.

Hide and Seek, Version II

Put your dog on a sit-stay or restrain him in one room. Allow him to see that you are taking treats with you. Hide from him in showers, closets, behind clothing, beds, anywhere. Once you are situated, call him. He will

have to search throughout the house for you. If he seems hopelessly lost, call his name quietly from time to time. Once he finds you, act happy and give him a treat and some loving. Remember, if you hide in a tree or any area off the ground, the dog will still be able to find you. Your scent drifts downward and actually pools in the area beneath you. Your dog will reach that spot, look up, and find you even though you haven't made a sound!

Find the Family's Children

This is an especially fun game if you have a big family. One day when your family is together, call the dog into the room. Check to see whether the dog has picked up on your children's names. Since you've been saying them over and over in front of him, he should know a couple and even the names of the other pets in the household. One person should say to the dog, "where's Paula?" You'll be amazed when the dog looks at the correct child. Repeat the exercise with each child's name.

If your dog simply wags his tail as he stares at you when you say a child's name, you'll have to educate him on these important matters. Have the correct child call the dog as you're saying that child's name. It's fine if he goes to that child. The child can even give the dog a treat. Work to a point where, when you say "where's Paula?" your child doesn't call the dog. The dog simply looks toward or goes to the child without being enticed. This exercise may take a few days. Most dogs will eventually catch on.

Once the dog connects the name with a particular child, have the child go farther and farther from you and the dog. When you ask the dog, "where's Paula?" he must go into another room to find her. To make the game more complicated, have the child hide. Take the dog into another room and say, "where's Paula?" The dog has internalized Paula's specific scent and so will use his great tracking skills to find that particular child. You can repeat this game with all the children.

Dog Races

A great way to burn up some of your dog's energy! This game can be played inside or outside. Take a small saucer and put it either in a room in the house or somewhere in the yard. The saucer makes the treat easier to see. With your dog on the leash, lead him to the plate and put a treat on it, but prevent him from getting it. Lead the dog away from the treat. When you stop, ask for a sit. The first few times you play this game, have your dog on a leash. In an excited way, say, "get the treat!" Run with your dog to the treat. You may have to use your "heel" command to get the dog to run with you. Eventually you can do this off-leash. Make sure you win sometimes. To keep the game challenging, he shouldn't win every time. If you have two dogs, you can have them race against each other. Put the saucer where the dogs can see it. Lead them both at least twenty feet away. Put them in a sit facing the treat. Say, "get it!" and watch them run for it. If one dog is faster than the

other, reward the slowpoke from time to time just for being a good sport. Widely published trainer Carol Lea Benjamin has taught her dogs to race to a ringing phone. That makes for a breathless hello.

Obstacle Course Race

In your yard or throughout your house, create a mock obstacle course. Set up a few chairs in your home or yard. Spy a table you'd like to go around or under. Find something both you and the dog can run over—an ottoman or a beanbag chair. Get a handful of treats and walk your dog through the course. That he performs "heel" well helps with this game. (In fact, this game will help him with that exercise.) For the first few passes, walk through the course with your dog, rewarding him from time to time with treats as he stays with you. Say, "good heel, good boy." The next day, go through the course, but go a little faster. Keep increasing the speed day by day until you are both racing through it. You don't even need to have an official obstacle course. Simply review your yard and furniture in your home and decide which way you're going to run. Eventually you and the dog will race over the obstacles like the best Olympians. You won't even need treats to entice him.

The Cookie Toss

One of the amazing things about dogs is that they can tell where a ball is going to land based on observing your hand position and the initial arc of the thrown object. For this game, make a short barrier between yourself and the dog. This can be a 2" x 8" board that is about eight feet long. If your dog is well trained, simply make a line on the floor with masking tape, but he must stay behind it. Every time he crosses that line, put him back over it and tell him to stay. If he continues to cross the line, refuse to participate in the game and ignore him. You can also play this game by placing the dog on the other side of a short fence.

Sit about eight feet on the other side of your barrier. Take a handful of treats. See how many he can catch in his mouth. As he catches each one, praise heartily. Angle your hand to the left and have him run that way. Once he's finished chewing, angle your hand to the right and toss the cookie in that direction. Keep him running back and forth. Make the treats small enough so that he doesn't spend a lot of time eating. It's also helpful for the dog if you look in the direction in which you expect the treat to land. If he's a good observational learner, he'll pick up these cues from your eye movements. If you can keep him running him back and forth as well as an accomplished tennis player does his opponent, you've come a long way in draining that incredible store of energy the dog has. The difficult part here is to keep the dog behind the line.

Multiple Retrieve

This game is modified from one of Ian Dunbar's PuppyDog Allstars K-9 Games. To play, the dog needs to enjoy retrieving. First, if you don't have a retrieve command, teach "take it," a command you can use to encourage your dog to take a toy from you and eventually retrieve toys from a distance. When playing with your dog, put a toy in his face and encourage him to take it, saying "take it" until he opens his mouth and takes it. Once he does, say "good take it!" and reward. You'll soon find that, whenever he comes to you to play and you say "take it," he'll look around for one of his squeakies.

To play a more exciting game than simple retrieve, put the dog's toys in one small area. Lead him away from the area and give your command, "take it!" He'll dash off to get one of the toys for you (especially if he hasn't seen you all day). Once he brings it back to you, take it and put it where he can't see it—on top of a table, into a box, etc. Praise and reward. If he doesn't readily drop the toy, hold a piece of food in front of his nose. To eat the food, he must drop the toy. As the toy falls, praise as if he deliberately dropped it, "good drop it!" Say, "take it" again and even point toward the pile of toys. If he seems bewildered, lead him to the area and put a toy in his face, encouraging him to take it. Once he does take it, say "good take it" and run back to where you were initially sitting. Soon he'll learn that he needs to retrieve all the toys in the area. Keep asking him to "take it" until he's brought back all of them. You can even time him to set him in a competition with himself. The key to this game is to keep saying "good boy!" when

he brings you a toy and then sending him off immediately with another "take it" command.

Retrieve with a Twist

If you're a sports person yourself, you can practice a few of your favorite activities and get the dog to help you. Take your softball and bat, tennis ball and racket, or your golf club and ball out to a park where dogs are allowed to run without leashes. First, throw whichever type of ball you choose for the dog to retrieve a few times. As you throw, say, "go!" When he brings it back to you, reward him with a treat. When you think the dog is ready, have him sit beside you. Say, "ready" to the dog and then hit your ball. As you hit the ball, say, "go!" He'll get quite a good run.

Basketball Roll

Because most dogs can't get hold of a ball as large as a basketball, they resort to pushing it and rolling it around with paws and nose. This challenge entrances many dogs because they can't get control of this ball as easily as they can all others. Dogs enjoy tackling large, out-of-control objects. Take a few large boxes and line them up across an area, leaving an open space about three feet wide so that two boxes are on one side of the space and two boxes are on the other side of the space. This space will be your goal. You might

want to secure these boxes by putting something heavy inside each. Let the dog play with the basketball for a little while. You start to play with the ball too, rolling it toward you and encouraging your dog to come after it. Start rolling the ball toward the open space, allowing the dog to paw at it as much as he wants. Eventually work the ball through the open space. The minute the dog pushes the ball through the space, say "goal!" and reward the dog profusely with treats and petting. Throw the ball back out into the area in front of your goal. Now, work the ball toward the goal again, saying "goal" a few times as you do so. Eventually you won't have to work with the dog. He'll start rolling the ball toward the goal himself to get the treat.

Treat Plant

With a handful of treats, take your dog into a room or one area of your yard. Have someone restrain the dog or put him in a stay. Plant the treats all over the room. After you're finished, this first time, let him go and say, "find 'em." Let him find the treats right then. If he needs help, lead him to the ones he's missed and help him find them. After the first encounter with this game, once you're done hiding treats, lead your dog out of the area and play with him somewhere else for a few minutes. Lead him back into the original area and say, "find 'em!" If he seems clueless, you may have to allow him to find the treats right after you hide them a few times.

Which Can Is It Under?

This game is modified from Terry Ryan's "The Shell Game" in her book *Games People Play to Train Their Dogs*. Carol Lea Benjamin also suggests a version of this game. Wash out three soup cans and get a handful of treats. Rub all three cans with the treat. If you don't, the dog will simply follow his super-sensitive nose to the correct can. We want to tax his memory, not his scent receptors. Sit opposite your dog and tell him to stay. Show him the treat in your hand. Put it under one of the cans and repeat your stay command. Mix the cans around while your dog watches. Stop moving the cans and say, "okay" or "get it!" Your dog will topple all cans trying to find the magic one.

Chase Me/Keep Away

Despite the fact that dogs love to chase each other, most owners don't participate in this game. We simply sit in a chair, throwing a ball repeatedly in one direction as if we have mechanical arms. Bring a brand new toy home from the store and squeak it in your dog's face a bit, but don't let him get it. Once he's really interested, run around your home or yard with it. Run in a circle. Change directions. Put an obstacle between the two of you. This is exactly how dogs love to play. Once the dog manages to get in front of you, let him have the toy. If he takes it and starts exploring it, refusing to run away from you, keep taking it. He'll learn he must keep running. Be careful

that you don't trip over the dog in this game! Once you've finished, don't let him have the new toy to chew in his leisure hours. That will only cause him to get bored with it. Unless you have a strongly prey-drive oriented dog, he won't chase you for some worn-out old toy.

Uncover Mommy!

Have your dog sit or restrain him. Grab a treat, lie on the floor, and put a blanket over yourself. You may want to protect your face with your hands. Call your dog. He will naturally want to get to you. As he struggles to get the blanket off of you, keep calling him. Eventually he will pull the blanket in the right way and you will be revealed. Once he does, reward him with a treat.

Spring Daddy!

Kids have fun with this one. Find a large cardboard box. If it's a refrigerator box, cut a doorway that you can easily get through. Situate the box in one room. Lead the dog into another room and have someone restrain him there or put him in a sit-stay. With a treat, climb into the box, shut the flaps (or door) and call your dog. He'll run and bombard the box, scratching all sides of it and making a big fuss. You may have to call him from inside the box. He'll have to get the flaps open or push through them. Once he gets to you, reward him.

You can advance this game by attaching a rope to the door and training him to pull on the rope to let you out. To show him how to open the door with the rope handle, stand outside the box and put a treat inside the box. Close the door. Shake the rope in his face so that he grabs the other end. Play tug-of-war with him for a bit and then let go. Since he was pulling, he'll pull the door open. Make sure the treat is easy to see. Let him have the treat inside.

Flyball

Flyball is actually a popular dog sport. There are many local clubs that sponsor flyball matches. However, you and your dog can have loads of fun playing with the flyball box yourselves. The box consists of an outside pedal, which when pressed by the dog releases a spring that shoots a ball into the

air on a horizontal trajectory. Depending on the flyball box, the ball flies between five and fifteen feet.

If this sounds like fun to you, think how tickled your dog will be. You need to train him to press the pedal, but that's not terribly difficult. Flyball boxes come with instructions. Your dog will also have to be over fifteen pounds to press the pedal successfully. The ball flies out and he must retrieve it. You can get a flyball box for about $40 at Dog-a-Polt by Burnett Designs at (206) 644-1288.

Frisbee

Like flyball, chasing a Frisbee flying disk has become a popular sport. If your speedy dog likes to jump, he would dig catching a Frisbee whether he got to do it in a show ring or your backyard. Dogs with short noses and those breeds prone to hip problems should probably find another sport to participate in. Whippets, greyhounds, Australian cattle dogs, and border collies excel at this sport, but any dog can participate.

Every year, Friskies PetCare Company, makers of Alpo dog food, puts on Canine Frisbee disc Championships. They suggest that you familiarize your dog with the Frisbee first by allowing him to eat treats or his dog food from it. Start to play tug of war with the Frisbee and allow him to get it from you on occasion. Then, toss the Frisbee with a friend. When the dog shows interest, gently toss it to him. Make sure to train the dog to bring the Frisbee back

to you. To encourage this, have plenty of treats ready after you throw. Kneeling down helps motivate the dog to return to you as well. To teach the dog to catch in midair, start by encouraging him to leap up and get the Frisbee as you hold it in your hand a few feet from the ground. Gradually hold it higher and higher. Allow him to take the Frisbee from you. Make small tosses in the air. You'll eventually progress until the dog is running out thirty feet and jumping high in the air.

Circus Dog Hoop-Jumping

This is a fun sport for small dogs who have lots of energy. A hula hoop or a bicycle tire serve well as hoops. You can also take a garden hose, cut it, shape it into a hoop and tape it in position with duct tape.

With your dog on his leash, pass one end of the leash through the hoop. The dog is now sitting on one side of the hoop and you are holding the end of the leash on the other side in your right hand. You should also put a treat in your right hand. Kneel down so that the dog sits a few feet to your left. Hold the hoop in your left hand so that the bottom of it is only two inches from the ground. Make sure that the dog is squarely facing the center of the hoop. Lean forward and peer at the dog through the hoop. Say, "hoop" and entice the dog through with the treat. If he is reluctant, gently guide him through with the leash. Do not allow him to go around the side of the hoop. If he jumps through, reward him lavishly.

Once he's coming through the hoop to you, you can gradually lift it higher off the ground. Do not repeat too many times in one training session. When the dog is able to jump his own height through the hoop held out to your left, transfer the hoop to your right hand and lower it to half the dog's height. (Do not raise the hoop height until your dog is at least fifteen months of age. Young ligaments don't respond well to strenuous jumping.) Encourage him to jump through this side. While you may think it's just as easy for him to jump through a hoop you're holding on the right, it's not. For most dogs, you need to start all over again when you change the hoop's position.

Eventually, you'll be able to hold the hoop in all positions and ask him to jump through it. Kneel down, putting one knee up so that your foot is flat on the ground. Place the hoop on your knee and give your command. Bend down, place the hoop on your back and give your command. The dog may need to get a foothold on your back to do this, so brace yourself. Lift the hoop until it's beside your waist and give your command. Eventually, you can work up a hoop-dancing routine with your dog set to music. If you have a dog who loves to jump, this is the ideal game for him.

Games for Dog Parties

These days people are getting together with their dogs to socialize. The many dog parks springing up reveal how much people want their dogs to play with same species pals. If you do manage to get together with some friends and

their dogs, here are some games you can all play together. Make sure you know the personalities of the dogs involved. Having unneutered males in the group is asking for trouble. If you plan to play a lot of group games, there are a few excellent books out. Roy Hunter's *Fun and Games with Dogs* includes many games that incorporate training. Terry Ryan's *Games People Play to Train Their Dogs* and *Life Beyond Block Heeling* also include many games for fun and training. You can order Ryan's books through Legacy by Mail at (800) 509-9814.

Musical Chairs

Count how many people will participate. Arrange in a circle the same number of chairs less one. You may want to space the chairs out so that the dogs don't get all tangled up with each other. All handlers should have their dogs on leashes. One person controls the music. When the music plays, handlers and dogs walk calmly around the chairs. When the music stops, handlers must find a chair and have their dogs sit in front of them facing them. If the dog doesn't sit, that person is out. Motivational treats are acceptable. A version of this game is played at the PuppyDog Allstars K-9 Games played all over the country. (More about the K-9 games is explained in Chapter 9.)

Zigzag Tail Wag

This game is modified from Terry Ryan's *Games People Play*. You'll need at least six people to play. Have people stand in two lines. The people should

not be standing directly opposite each other, but midway between the two opposite them so that if a line ran from the first person to the last person, it would form a zigzag. The first person in line should restrain the dog. The second person calls the dog, "Dog, come" then pets and rewards the dog once he does. The third person calls the dog and does the same. This continues on down the line. This games helps your dog feel more comfortable with strangers.

Squeaky Toys No More!

Well, it doesn't have to be that drastic. Squeaky toys do serve their purpose. It's just that their limited complexities get discovered pretty quickly. The toys below stimulate more than most.

Ball on a Stick

Pet stores sell them, but you can easily make one. This toy consists of a one- to two-foot dowel with a hole drilled through one end. A nylon cord about six feet long passes through the hole and is knotted. The other end of the string is then threaded through a tennis ball. You can whip the ball back and forth or manipulate it by pulling the cord through the dowel. Dogs love both the fact that you are attached to the toy and that the toy is moving in a crazy configuration. Even the most lethargic dog jumps for this toy.

Roping Favorite Toys

Tie a cord at least eight feet long to the handle of a plastic milk jug or rolled towel. By manipulating the rope, you can make both objects move in erratic patterns. Again, with this type of toy, the dog gets to satisfy that drive to chase and capture erratically moving prey.

Buster Cube

We talked about the Buster Cube in Chapter 5, but in case any of you are skipping, we want to mention it again. It's a six-inch plastic square with a small opening on one side. You pour small pellets of dry food through this opening. The inside is divided into several compartments that prevent the pellets from pouring out all at once. The dog must roll the Cube around with his paws and nose to release the food one piece at a time. You can find it in the pet supply catalogs or by asking your local pet store to order it.

Colorless Plastic Bottles

Emptied and carefully cleaned mouthwash and shampoo bottles make very exciting toys if you allow your dog to play on the rug. Watch how the bottle comes to life as the dog tries to stop it from slipping across the floor. The pressure of his paw makes it slip, slide, and bump off furniture. Make sure your dog doesn't chew it so much that he's able to break off pieces and swallow them. Don't leave this type of chewable toy for your dog when he's unsupervised.

Ice Cubes on a Linoleum Floor

Here's another safe item that will give your prey-driven dog lots to chase. Like the bottles above, the minute the dog paws the ice cube, it slips away. Once he's done playing with it, he can have fun crunching it up. The only mess you're left with is a little water. To stay safe, don't encourage your dog to chase the ice cubes if he doesn't seem inclined to do so. He may be nervous about running across the wet floor. Let him make up his own mellow ice cube game. On the other hand, some dogs don't mind sliding and crashing about. These dogs will have a great time pawing that slippery ice cube over the linoleum.

The Wrestling Opponent

When your dog was a pup, he and his siblings tumbled around as they wrestled. About the same size, they were formidable opponents for each other. It's not a surprise then that the squeaky toys he has now underwhelm him. Give your dog a big box that's at least as high as his shoulder or a big stuffed animal to wrestle with. He'll roll over this large object, butt it with his head, and try to stand on it to assert his dominance. He'll have a great time shaking it. Stuffed animals won at carnivals and old pillows serve well. Don't expect either a stuffed animal or a large cardboard box to last too long as a wrestling partner! Yes, it's a bit messy, but it's better than cleaning up pieces of your sofa.

Irrational Balls

Balls that wobble and bounce in unpredictable ways are more stimulating to dogs than the traditional, one-trajectory ball. The Wobbler and the Space Ball give dogs a good workout and challenge. The Kong toys also give a good, unpredictable bounce because of their shape. The toys come in many different sizes. Be sure to choose a size your dog cannot swallow. When pieces start to be chewed off, discard the toy.

Hi-Ho, Hi-Ho, It's Off to Camp We Go...

If you want games galore, consider taking your dog to a dog camp. There, the decisions about games are left up to the staff, who also must organize the

equipment and playing field. Playing games with other dogs makes the whole thing more fun.

Camp Winnaribbun

Located in Lake Tahoe, Nevada, Camp Winnaribbun offers hikes, Frisbee competitions, and health lectures, as well as training classes in agility, flyball, tracking, and herding. You and your dog can even get private lessons. For $650, they'll feed, board, and entertain you and your dog for a week. For a brochure, write to Camp Winnaribbun, P. O. Box 50300, Reno NV, 89513, or call (702) 747-1561.

Camp Gone-to-the-Dogs

Remember the Macarena? The popular dance all the kids were doing? Well, dogs can do it, too. Camp Gone-to-the-Dogs helped one class of owners and their dogs learn this fun dance. Beyond the latest line dances, Camp Gone-to-the-Dogs offers classes in all competitive areas. When the pups are snoozing, veterinarians and behaviorists provide lectures about various topics. There are two summer camps and one fall camp. For more information, you can access their web site at http://camp-gone-tothe-dogs.com. You can also write to the camp at RR1 Box 958, Putney VT, 05346, or call director Honey Loring at (802) 387-5673.

Dog camps that focus on specific competitive sports also exist. Local obedience clubs can help you locate these advanced camps.

In Conclusion...

Remember the day you finally put away Chutes & Ladders to play big games like Monopoly and Risk? That was a good day. Similarly, entertaining a dog can be more invigorating than throwing a tennis ball over and over. Been there. Done that. The games in this chapter help to reanimate a bored and unchallenged dog. You'll find that the two of you will make modifications to the games to suit your own play style. Have fun! Didn't you get your dog as a big toy anyway?

7
Get That Dog a Job!

Most evenings your dog sleeps the hours away, his heavy head pinioning your foot, his drool seeping into your sock. He doesn't know that while he slumbers, you're reading this book. His sleeping hours are numbered.

Having a daily task to perform keeps the dog's mind active. Even human brain researchers concur: people over fifty engaged in interesting work tend to be less forgetful. Beyond the intellectual benefits, training your dog to complete a task strengthens the bond between the two of you. Most domestic dogs were bred to work in conjunction with humans. Most enjoy listening for our commands and carrying them out to the best of their ability. (That said, know that there are those who hold no other gods before them-

selves.) They also relish the goodies they get for a job well done. As we mentioned before, training a dog for ten minutes can tire him just as much as taking him for a thirty-minute walk. He loves his walk, but as the two of you stroll along, you're not really interacting as much as you do when you train together. Your dog wants your direct attention, and giving him a job is one way you can provide that.

But what kind of job is your dog cut out for? Skip the skills inventory tests and focus on his drives and his body size. Big dogs can carry packs and pull carts, which are both fun, useful activities. Retrievers like to bring things back to you. Terriers love to chase. German shepherds, Australian cattle dogs, and border collies get a big kick out of rounding up other people and animals. In this chapter, we will again use the markers introduced on page 93 to indicate which aspect of intelligence each job emphasizes.

Pick Up Your Toys!

If you've been following this book carefully, you've gone out and blown the mortgage money on a variety of fun toys. Good dog owner! No house to live in, but you've got a dog smarter than the tenth-grader who used to live next door. The result, however, is a living room full of vinyl vegetables with eyes, creatures from Dr. Moreau's lab, and a few bumpy mutations of balls. Who's going to pick up those things? Not you. You're busy making doggy's goodie bag for the next day.

On your command, your dog can pick up his toys and put them away. Of course, you'll need some sort of toy box to help him out. Make sure the toy box is a few inches lower than his muzzle so that he can easily drop the toys. Teaching the dog to pick up his toys takes three steps: retrieving, dropping, and going away from you to drop.

1. Retrieving an object.

Many dogs automatically retrieve. But to attach a command to it is another story. When you play fetch or catch with your dog, start saying "take it!" as he goes after the ball. Now, hold an object in front of his face and say "take it!" If he won't take it readily, hold onto his collar and wait for him to open his mouth. You can also cheat by rubbing food on the object. The minute he opens his mouth, pop the object in. Praise lavishly: "good take it! good boy!" This is a game. Stay excited and happy to make it fun for the dog.

2. Dropping.

To get the dog to let go of an object he's holding, put a treat in front of his nose and say "drop." When he opens his mouth to get the treat, the object will drop out. Praise with "good drop, good boy." Once your dog learns to drop on command, add a detail, "box." When the dog has the object in its mouth, lead him to his toy box. Say "drop, box." Once he drops the toy, make a big fuss and reward him with a treat.

3. Picking up scattered toys.

When the toys lie scattered around the room/yard like casualties from a great party, put your dog on the leash, lead him to each toy, and say "take it." When he picks up the toy, lead him to the toy box, saying "good take it" over and over. You may have to pick a few toys up at first and hold them under his nose. Once the toy is over the box, say "drop, box." After you've lead him through this a few times, take off his leash and sit by the box. Look toward a toy that's close and say, "take it." He'll probably come to you with it. Guide his muzzle over the box and say, "drop, box." Once he's finished, reward him and then give him the "take it" command again. Move farther and farther from the box until you're directing the dog from a distance of fifteen feet.

Once your dog gets the hang of this job, you'll have to direct him, saying "take it" and "drop, box" several times. Give him treats intermittently. After he has put three toys in the box, give him a treat. Then after he's put two toys in, reward him.

Light My Pipe and Then Go Fetch My Slippers... Keys, Purse, Newspaper...

Retrieval skills are once again required in this occupation. Hold whatever object you want him to take under his muzzle. If you use your newspaper,

say, "take it, paper!" Once he takes it in his mouth, pet and praise him, "good paper! good boy!" Tell him to "drop" and reward him with a treat. Again, if he's reluctant to take it, hold him by the collar and wait for his mouth to open a bit. Pop the object into his mouth and then go into hysterical praise.

When teaching these job skills, stay in the area where the object usually is and leave this object in one place. A newspaper usually lands in about the same spot every day. Slippers usually sit in one corner of a closet, and keys should be kept in one area as well. If you're training the dog to retrieve the paper from the driveway, it's likely that you'll be putting on a show for the neighbors for a while. If you're training the dog to retrieve your purse, keep it on one chair and train right in that area. Once the dog is willingly taking the object, you can move a few feet away from it. As you sit that few feet away, tell him, "take it, paper." Once he approaches you with it, tell him to drop it and reward him with a treat. (Remember not to train too many times or the dog will get bored and decide training is no fun.) Move farther away and give your command "take it, paper." As the dog picks up the object and starts to return to you, say "good boy, good paper!" Dogs should be praised while they're carrying out the requested action. Eventually, you can open your front door, give your command and watch the dog brave the elements while you stay warm and toasty in the house.

The Furry Courier

Not talking to your spouse? You don't
need a child to act as go-between. Your
dog can learn to take objects and notes
to the other members of your household. Marital battles aside, this task
can be quite useful if you both you and
your spouse work out of your home.
You've already taught him "take it" so
that he knows how to carry something.

Strap a comfortable pack on your dog, and you can send even more things
(and these will arrive slobberless!). If you train carefully, your dog will eventually learn how to take objects to different individuals in the house.

All people involved have to work on this one. Stand about six feet away
from your partner and call your dog. Put an object in front of your dog's
mouth and tell him to "take it." Once he's got a good hold on it, say "go to
Daddy!" At the same time, your partner should be calling the dog, "Dog,
come!" Once the dog takes the object to your partner, your partner tells the
dog to drop it and then rewards him with affection and treats. Your partner
then puts an object in front of the dog's face and tells him to take it. The dog
is instructed to "go to Mommy!" at which point you call the dog back to you.
(Of course, you can call your partner by name if you aren't comfortable
being a canine "Mommy.")

Increase the distance between yourself and your partner until your partner is in another room. Eventually, your partner won't need to call the dog when you give the command, "go to Daddy!" If you have a real Caninestein, he'll learn the names of everyone in the household and be able to take the object to whichever recipient you indicate.

Pulling a Sled, Bag of Leaves, Etc.

A day's yard work gives homeowners a great sense of satisfaction. Until, that is, we look at the mountain of leaf-filled garbage bags we've erected. And where was the dog the entire time? Watching happily, as usual. Now it's time for him to work.

You can tie a rope to a bag of leaves and have your dog help you pull the twenty bags to the trash. The trick here is getting the dog to pull for a distance. Don't tie the rope onto the bag yet. First, play with your dog with a two- to three-foot piece of it. You can also throw the rope and tell the dog to "take it" if you've successfully taught that command. Now, tie the rope to a bag of leaves or any other refuse you need hauled a short distance. Walk about ten feet away from the bag. Tell your dog to "take it!" He will want to bring the rope to you so the two of you can play with it. Encourage him once he takes it in his mouth with "good boy!" As he moves toward you, say "come! good boy!" Slowly move backwards toward your destination, encour-

aging him to follow you with your "come!" command. Once he gets to the curb or garbage area, say "drop it!"

If your dog is reluctant to pull the bag when it's full, you can take the intermediate step of tying the rope to an empty bag after playing with the rope by itself. Let the dog run around the yard holding onto the rope. If he insists on mauling the bag, he may not be a good candidate for garbage hauler.

Bring Your Dish

In their book *Dog Tricks*, Carol Lea Benjamin and Captain Arthur J. Haggerty describe how to get your dog to bring his dish to you at dinnertime. It's best to use a plastic dish that's easy for the dog to grab. The first step is to entice the dog to grab the dish. First, shake it in front of his face, much as you do when you're encouraging him to play with a toy. Then, toss the dish. When your dog grabs it and brings it to you, reward him by putting a treat in it and let him eat it. Keep tossing the dish. As the dog is en route back to you with it, say, "bring your dish! good, bring your dish!" When he gets to you and drops it, praise and reward with treats. Repeat that exercise several times until he understands it clearly. On a new day, take your dog into the area where the dish is. Ask him to bring his dish before you lay a finger on it. Help him out by looking at the dish. Benjamin and Haggerty say that you

might have to shake the treat box for him. He knows by now that the treats are associated with bringing the dish.

Round Up the Kids

One way people control a dog that likes to bark is to teach him to bark on command. With this behavior-control technique, the dog gets to bark, but you have some control over when he does so. If your kids play out in the street or the field, inform them that you'll be teaching the dog to bark at them when they are to come in. Your children's positive response to the dog will reinforce his behavior.

Have your children get the dog into whatever state causes him to bark. They can wind him up with play or come to the door and ring the doorbell. Be close by so that when the dog does bark, you can jump right in with your, "speak!" command. Reward with treats and say, "good boy! good speak!" It's important that the children (or whomever you want the dog to eventually summon) elicit the bark. The bark will be directed toward them. You may have to trick him into barking in this way several times before the dog makes the connection between his behavior and your command.

To make things easier, use one of the children's names so the dog first looks in that direction. (Study the game Find the Family's Children in Chapter 6 to learn how to direct the dog's attention to another family member.)

First say the name and then give your speak command. Once the dog goes to the children and barks, have the children reward him with treats and praise, and you step in and reward him as well. Say one child's name and then give your speak command. Now, put more and more distance between yourself and the children. Say a child's name and "speak!" Reward the dog for leaving you and going toward the children to bark. Remember to have them reward him as well.

Now, start putting the children in one room and lead the dog into another room with you. Say a child's name and give your speak command, "where's Paula? speak!" When the dog goes into the other room and barks, have the children reward him. You come in and reward him as well. Eventually, you'll be able to open the door, tell your dog the child's name and watch as he runs out and barks them in from the evening's neighborhood play.

Carting

If you have little children or grandchildren and a big dog, carting could provide a lot of entertainment for everyone. Parade appearances are the big purpose in life for training a dog to cart, but there are practical uses as well. Dogs with carts can help clean up the yard, haul trash down to the road, walk to the store, and many other hauling jobs that make your life a little easier.

The breeds who most commonly cart are large dogs like Newfoundlands, Great Pyrenees, Bernese mountain dogs. However, any size dog can cart. We have known carting shelties, Scotties and even Chihuahuas! Coauthor Betty Fisher even has a carting bulldog. Carts from toy stores can be adapted for dogs. Design a nylon or leather harness for your dog and have your local shoe shop stitch it together. Add the appropriate hardware and you're all set. Too much work? A free catalog for equipment is available from Dog Works, Inc. at (800) 787-2788. They carry equipment for carting as well as for water sports, tracking, backpacking, and sledding.

Dogs who pull their carts well often participate in competitions where they can earn the title "Draft Dog." A local kennel or appropriate breed club will be able to tell you where and when carting classes and competitions are

being held. These carting classes can help you teach your dog to pull a cart for any activity you envision. To find your local breed club, call the American Kennel Club at (919) 233-9767 or visit their home page at http://www.akc.org.

Packing Dogs

Some dogs make their living carrying smaller objects in packs. Using dog packs, your dog can carry tools, supplies, his own food, and many other things. One company president equipped his West Highland white terrier with a double-sided pack and set him about delivering the mail. A geologist in Nevada trained his German shorthaired pointer to carry hammers and picks between different members of the field team using a pack.

Wearing the pack, the dog simply needs to know where to go, a feat that's not too tough to train. The person you want the dog to go to can either call the dog or you can teach your dog to be a Furry Courier with the "go to" command as described in the exercise above. Wolf Packs LLC makes water-repellent nylon packs for dogs to carry their own water or food, even tools. For a catalog, send $1 to Wolf Packs LLC, 755 Tyler Creek Road NW, Ashland OR, 97520-9408.

Many outdoor lovers have begun equipping their dogs with packs and venturing into the wild together. Most well-conditioned working breeds and

athletic mid-sized dogs can carry about 33 percent of their body weight. If you and your dog are just beginning hiking, have the dog carry a low weight for a short distance. A former backyard snoozer cannot become an Indian brave overnight. He must be conditioned. There is also a nice web site that covers backpacking with your dog in depth: http:/snapple.cs.washington. edu/canine/backpacking.

Is Acting Work? The Hollywood Dog

In the larger cities, talent agencies are waiting for your dog's head shots. These days, dogs often get as many laughs as the movie heroes and sitcom characters to whom they play sidekick. Most diva dogs are raised and trained on Holly-wood "farms" that house many potential stars at once. However, with the growing popularity television and big-screen dog stars enjoy, more producers and advertisers are turning to household pets for the next Lassie.

Camera One Canine Actors, a San Diego animal talent agency, has placed regular folks' dogs in movies and television shows, as well as many Alpo and Science Diet commercials. These dogs can do such things as take a note to another person, retrieve their food bowls, pretend they're playing the piano, turn on the television, ride skateboards, and scratch on command, among other tricks. Coauthor Betty Fisher's white bulldog, Storm, made such a stunning debut in Chuck Norris' *Top Dog* that Italian designers were calling to offer their dresses for her portly appearance at the Oscars.

Sometimes, if the talent agencies like the look of your dog, they'll go to the trouble of training him for specific exercises. In fact, there's usually a dog trainer on staff. Nevertheless, the most impressive dog already performs a number of charming tricks. Most agencies like to see that you and your dog have been to an obedience school with a good reputation and that your dog can perform a reliable sit.

Because light-colored dogs photograph better, not too many Doberman pinschers, Rottweilers, Newfoundlands, or Labrador retrievers are found among the ranks of the Screen Actors' Guild. These days, agencies are most eager for Dalmatians, Jack Russell terriers, golden retrievers, and Shih Tzus.

Getting your dog a break may not be as time-consuming as Hollywood myths perpetuate. Either look up "Animal Rental," "Animal Brokers," or "Talent Agencies" in the yellow pages to find agencies that handle dogs. Ask whether the agency is licensed with the United States Department of Agriculture. That the agency was screened by the USDA will help your peace of mind. Send each appropriate agency a description of your dog and his training, along with a good head shot, a body shot, and a photo of him doing something charming. Professional photographers can best reflect what your dog has to offer. Since many photographers specialize in pets, look until you find a experienced one. You can dress the dog. In fact, since some commercials now require the dog to wear something, having a photo of your dog in clothing may prove a plus. You should also send a history of the dog's obedience work and a list of the tricks he can perform. Be prepared— casting agents do not focus solely on the dog. They're looking at the neurosis level of the owner as well. Agents don't want their producer-clients to suffer from the nail-biting of hyperprotective stage parents.

Actually, owners don't need to be too worried about the well-being of their up-and-coming star on the set. On every production, the law requires that a representative from the American Humane Association is present to make sure that all animals are well rested, exercised, fed, and watered. Also, on every show, a dog trainer oversees the animals. Ever since a stunt man rode a horse off a seventy-foot cliff during the filming of *Jesse James* in 1938, producers and directors have been cautious about caring for all animals involved.

Despite a film crew's best intentions, however, sometimes owners who stay on the set find their dogs' needs being overlooked. Amidst the frantic pace of a take, dogs have been left in hot sun for longer than owners like. Fights have broken out between two dogs who were accidentally left unre-

strained. If you feel your dog is not getting the treatment you had expected and your complaints are being ignored, be prepared to walk off the set with the dog. While most Hollywood dogs receive star pampering, you want to be on hand to make sure your dog receives this treatment.

Whoa! Stop those dreams of financial independence delivered through your pup's good looks! Payment for a day on the set is about $450. Without unions, dogs haven't been able to win residuals. If you get a commercial, expect to receive about $125 per hour. These fees seem reasonable, but after the agency siphons off a hefty portion and can only get you one gig per year, you've got to be in it for love. Beware of agencies that charge up-front fees. Their only fees should be in the form of the commission they receive from your pet's work. This rate runs from between 10 and 25 percent.

In Conclusion...

Your dog doesn't need to be a loafer. Whether his life's calling is to be a great retriever of newspapers or a swift and dependable courier, he can tackle minor duties. Since he'll probably only work part time, you won't have to worry about sick days or job burn-out. What's more, your dog's job performance will dazzle friends and neighbors whose pets have degenerated into doorstops. With a job, a dog takes more of an interest in life. Trainers and dog lovers report that employed dogs are much more alert and playful than the canines of leisure that inhabit most households.

8
Tips for Creating Time and Space in Your Life for Your Dog

If you and your dog could enjoy all of the sports and games in this book together, his life would be a carnival. But you never signed up to be a carny; you already have a job. Dogs don't require constant entertainment. If they did, the wild dogs of the plains would have migrated to cruise ships, not people's homes. Remember that Vegas-style shows, endless buffets, and tours aren't really a dog's idea of fun. One of the reasons dogs have adapted well to the human species is that they can handle the amount of time we are unable

to pay attention to them. Most active in the morning and evening, both domestic and wild canines snore away while humans toil.

In fact, a dog will sleep a good part of the day away even if you religiously make your goodie bags and fill your yard with agility equipment. Before you dial your shrink, realize *this one is not your fault*. Research veterinarians at Cornell University point out that dogs are only sporadically active. Even hard-working sled dogs spend as much as 80 percent of a twenty-four-hour period just resting. In one study, dogs in a laboratory setting rested 75 percent of the time. Clearly, hours and hours of sleep go into every dog on the canine assembly line. If you overwhelm your dog with a Yuppie-inspired play and activity schedule, he'll burn right out and you will, too.

But how do we know what level of challenge our dog needs? The levels differ. Young dogs need more than older dogs. Some breeds are more demanding than others. Those in the working group—retrievers, shepherds, pointers—may be more anxious for you to provide some fun. One way to get an idea about your dog's need for challenge is to observe the objects he chooses to destroy. Cornell veterinarians found that a dog that attacks chewable and easily moved objects such as pillows or pencils may exhibiting "exploratory behavior." In other words, he's looking for something new to do, smell, taste, and touch because he's bored with what he has.

On the other hand, the destructive dog who chews through door frames or windows doesn't suffer from the malaise of ennui. He just can't stand being separated from his owner. This nervous guy's trying to get through the

last barrier he believes remains between himself and beloved Daddy or Mommy. Separation anxiety is a complicated syndrome that must be handled carefully. A few of the suggestions in this book can help relieve it. The goodie bag or treat-filled box given at the time of departure can distract a dog from the pain of separation. Whether the dog is destroying from boredom or separation anxiety, some food-enhanced toys or a sporadic radio broadcast can help get him through the day. Preparing him for this period by spending energy-burning quality time with him before you leave can also alleviate destructive behavior. If your dog chews, analyze the objects he loves to get his teeth around to determine his needs.

Even though the dog will rest up to 75 percent or eighteen hours of his day, those six hours that he's alert should be good ones. With a decent environment to explore, car trips, a few exciting games, and training, your dog will enjoy a much more fulfilling life than most.

However, squeezing in even these activities can strain an already overburdened schedule. Here are a few ways to make your dog's care a little easier on you.

The Truth about Training

Most people are overwhelmed when they think about the time and energy required to train their dogs. They envision needing to spend two hours a day, five days each week in order to create a well-mannered dog. That image

would prompt anybody to shy away from training manuals or even attempt to teach the sit. The truth is that after you've initially taught an exercise, your dog can become a decent citizen if you spend only ten to twenty minutes two to three times a week reinforcing it. We're not going for Olympians here. No eight-hour practices followed by a three-hour workout on the Nautilus machines. It's true that the initial training period to teach a new task requires a little more time—perhaps five twenty-minute sessions each week. But most dogs catch on pretty quickly—often within a few days. Before you know it, you're spending only fifteen minutes on Tuesdays, Thursdays, and Saturdays teaching your dog the most complicated of tricks and exercises.

Fast and Efficient Training

When you train, if you are persistent and consistent, the dog will learn exercises faster, saving you both time and energy. Train in small increments. Praise and reinforcement of correct behavior works better than correcting the incorrect response. Even if you have to place a dog with leash or hands in a correct position, remember to reward and praise the instant he does what you want. It doesn't matter what it took to get him to the correct position. He deserves his reward.

In Play, Ten Minutes Is All It Takes

Most people guiltily ignore their dogs because they think their demands will be so great, they'll be overwhelmed. If they start a game of fetch, the

game will go on for an hour. That's not the case. According to San Diego behaviorist, Dr. Patrick Melese, ten minutes of direct attention can go a long way in satisfying a dog. For dogs who spend the day alone, taking ten minutes in the morning to play with him will help him feel more calm and content throughout the ten hours he's separated from you. It will even help him curb his beaverish appetite for table legs and shoes. Spending a solid ten minutes in the morning with him is doubly important if he doesn't have a morning walk. Throughout your evening, play with him in ten minute spurts. In between, have Gumabone and rawhide chews available for him to mellow out with.

To adapt this ten-minute guide to the games and jobs in this book, teach one part of each activity at a time. It's fine to stop the exercise before the dog has entirely mastered it, but try to make sure he understands a component of it before you quit. For instance, to teach the Hide and Seek Game, spend one of your ten-minute sessions teaching the dog to come to you for food. Stay in the area where he can see you. Do that a few times and then start hiding. Don't stop calling him to you until he comes to you consistently. You'll soon find that although you planned on spending ten minutes, thirty minutes flew by without you even noticing.

Options

Send Your Dog to Spend the Day with a Dog Friend

At 5:30, your long day finally ends. As you walk in the door, your dog springs from the floor to the ceiling over and over again. You realize that his day has just begun. He's ready for a walk, playing, grooming, any kind of attention you can give him—and lots of it, please. But what if you and your dog dragged in together? You had a long day at the office; he had a long day, too, but with Barky, next door. You both get something to eat and then crash in front of the television set.

If your dog barks from loneliness during the day, listen in your neighborhood for other dogs that are barking, too. Chances are their owners have the same concerns. Approach these other owners and suggest that your dogs meet each other. Introduce the two on neutral territory such as in the street between your houses. Make sure they get along. *(Caution: an unneutered male is a tough match for any other dog.)* Then, on Monday and Wednesday take your dog to the other dog's home so they can spend the day together. On Tuesday and Thursday, have the neighbor dog come to your home or backyard. The two can play, explore together, groom each other, and double-team the postman. If you feel a little shy about approaching your neighbor, think again. A 1995 Hallmark cards survey found that 67 percent of pet owners carry their pet's photo in their wallet and 75 percent celebrate their pet's birthday. You're not the only mushball out there.

Variety

While dogs usually like strict routine, doing the same thing every night gets boring for you. You want to think of your dog as a fun outlet, not a tiresome burden. Otherwise, he may end up like so many others—in the pound. During the time you typically spend with him, interchange walking with playing or training. Some evenings take your walk. On others, spend twenty minutes just playing or training. As we mentioned, these mental activities will tire your dog as efficiently as physical ones.

Plan and Prepare When You Have the Most Energy

Some of us are night owls. Others shine in the morning. Think about which part of the day you have the most clarity and energy. At that time, decide which game or training exercise you'd like to engage your dog in that day. Set out the equipment you'll need. When you get home, you don't have to spend the mental energy making yet another decision. You can simply enjoy the brainless time you'll spend with a creature that adores you unreservedly.

Divide and Conquer Tasks

Involve the whole family in the care of the dog. Tell them that it's everyone's responsibility to provide a meaningful life for the animal they took steps to bring into their lives. Because children like to have some control over their tasks, make a list of the several games and activities and have each

person choose which one he or she would like to be responsible for. A child as young as seven can begin teaching simple commands. One child may have the goal of teaching the dog to jump over an agility jump. Another child could make it his job to play hide and seek with the dog. By picking an activity they would most enjoy, children will be more likely to devote themselves to it. Working together, the whole family can teach the dog each member's name (see The Furry Courier in Chapter 7). Engaging the whole family lifts the burden from you and gives everyone a common interest.

Drive to the Dog Park

How about this scenario? You drive home, get your dog into the car, and drive down to the local dog park. You stand at the sidelines with other owners while your dog romps freely with the only companions that can truly wear him out—other dogs. As the dogs tear around the park, you and other owners talk casually about your pet's age, breed, and bizarre behaviors. Not too challenging for you, but a rollercoaster of fun for your dog.

Locate the local dog parks in your area by calling your parks and recreation department. Over the last few years, many dog owners have successfully lobbied to have a few park hours dedicated to off-leash time for dogs. Other cities, such as Poway, California, have created elaborate dog parks,

complete with fenced-in areas, water buckets, and plastic clean-up bags. Here the dogs can romp freely, while owners enjoy a relaxing, spontaneous dog show.

The Dog Area

Keep one corner of the kitchen or garage cabinets for dog equipment. Cartons for toys, cartons for treats and chews, and a hook to hang leashes. Keeping everything in one area reduces the confusion and irritation of having a disorganized pile of dog equipment. Buy toys and other paraphernalia when it's on sale and store it the dog area. Have a carton for the toys you rotate out of the dog's life for a few months. When you go to give them back to him, he'll think they're new (see Chapter 5).

The Training Buddy

Studies have shown that people who have a workout partner often exercise more. Similarly, if you know another dog owner who's trying to train or challenge their dog, join forces. Take your dogs to the park together and work on different commands. Have your dogs play games together: hide and seek or races work well for several dogs looking for some action.

Fun, Local Classes

If your family isn't really into the dog, other students at local classes will gladly swap corny dog stories with you. Signing up for local classes gets you

and the dog out with others. If the sound "obedience" makes you yawn, look further for beginning classes in Agility, Flyball, Frisbee, Musical Freestyle, Ian Dunbar's Puppy AllStars K-9 Games, or any of the dog sports appropriate for your dog's breed. These more exciting ways to train will amuse and entertain both you and your dog.

Errand Dog

Use the old two-things-at-once time-saving trick. To get the dog out and about, stimulating his mind with new sights, sounds, and smells, consider taking him with you on your errands. Call the places you commonly go and ask if they allow pets in. The post office, home supply stores, and many other stores allow pets. The dog will love the ride in the car and the chance to see new places and people. Even some restaurants allow diners' dogs to sit somewhere near them.

To make it more convenient, leave your pet safety transportation equipment in the car. Consider the doggy seat belts available in the pet supply stores. Small dogs also have their own version of a car seat. The Lookout car seat is a box with a lined soft bedding and exterior that you can snap into the car seat belt. It's high enough to allow your pet to see out while safely fastened to the seat belt and harness. For $55.00, the Lookout car seat is yours from O'Donnell Industries at (800) 635-9755. O'Donnell Industries also makes the Pet Rider Bicycle Seat which attaches to the front or back or any bicycle. There is also a dog version of the baby Snugli (a pack that holds

the baby on your chest) called Pac a Pet. For about $35.00, small dogs can go around with you strapped safely to your chest. Call (208) 853-4845 for more information.

Your large dog will just have to go in your backseat or hatch. A gate that divides the hatch area from the rest of the car will cost you around $50. To further save yourself some trouble, keep an old blanket in the car to cover the seats so that you don't get overwhelmed with dog odor and hair. There are many odor-neutralizing products on the market now that will keep your car and living area smelling fresh.

And When You Can't Take It Anymore...

Been fantasizing about putting him in a kennel for a few days? Here's the permission you need: boarding your dog for a couple of days will do him good. Truly. Veterinarians warn that dogs should become accustomed to being penned in a strange place. Vets often see an injured animal come in that has never spent a night away from Mommy and Daddy. After the treatment or surgery, some of these animals die—not as a result of their injuries, but from the stress they experience from being separated from home and placed in the recovery kennel. The strange sounds, smells, and noises combined with his physical trauma can literally give your pet a heart attack. To prepare him for the unexpected, expose him to a kennel situation when he's in good health. Your dog will learn that he will be fed and taken care of in a

kennel. If you need a break from all his demands, drop him at that kennel and don't look back (at least for a day or two.)

In Conclusion...

Trainer Carol Schatz warns people considering a dog to be ready to spend a quarter of the amount of time and energy that you would expect to spend with a human child. You probably didn't know this rule before you got your dog. Now—after tending to his playing, feeding, grooming, socializing, training, and walk time—you've learned it very well. A dog's demands can feel overwhelming. Joining forces with others, whether a dog-loving friend, people in the dog park, or other students in local classes, alleviates some of the tension involved in caring for a dog. And when a local kennel can take over for a day or two, you'll both come back refreshed and ready to play.

9
Building Big, Bulging Brains with Fun, Unusual Dog Activities

Many a dog owner never gets past the basic puppy classes where the dog learns how to put his bottom on the ground. Bored, we discard the whole class idea before realizing that other structured training activities—although a bit harder to find—can be much more fun. As we've mentioned countless times, good training challenges your dog's mind and body. It gives him goals to strive for, problems to solve, and choices to make. Unfortunately, unless

there's a dominance problem, most dogs comprehend "sit," "down," and "come" faster than they learn the meaning of the can opener.

Don't think you're the first one to become bored and disenchanted with obedience training. Bored folks just like you have been spending a few years organizing activities that incorporate obedience, but have bigger, more exciting goals. Because these activities are just beginning to get some recognition, the time to get in on them is now. Remember, you don't have to compete. View these recreations as the canine version of Mommy & Me classes. Your dog's mind and health will benefit from challenge and novelty they provide, even if you two never set foot in a showring.

Agility

Imagine: tunnels to dodge through, balance beams to navigate, teeter totters to slap to the ground—all of these big toys can be part of your dog's life when you begin training in agility. Dog experts are raving about the benefits of agility training. Why? In the process of teaching your dog to steer himself through all of this equipment, he learns stay, come, sit, down—all of the obedience commands that make him bearable to live with. However, now he does these things joyfully because, as most who train in agility realize, *the dog loves this stuff!* Shy, introverted dogs gain self-confidence, and clumsy, lumbering dogs begin to float like Baryshnikov (well okay…they run into fewer doors).

There are many different pieces of agility equipment that the dog eventually learns to cross, crawl through, climb over, and collapse upon. In an official agility trial, up to twenty are set up in a complicated course. No two courses are alike. The dog runs through the course directed by the owner, who shouts commands as he struggles to stay alongside the dog. Often, two pieces of agility equipment are placed close together so that the dog must listen carefully to the owner to know which one to go to. Clearly, this process taxes a dog's brain (in a good way).

But that's for the competitors. *You don't have to compete!* Agility trainers happily welcome those who have no intention of winning ribbons. In fact, your dog doesn't even have to be an obedience-school graduate to start in agility. Most agility classes are small enough to ensure that the instructor can pay attention to individual problems. Think of it as structured play time for your dog, with someone else shouldering the responsibility of games director. Also, participating in this sport provides you a chance to get outdoors with other dog lovers, away from the daily responsibilities of your life. Send your spouse with your child to soccer practice. Take the dog to agility.

Any size or breed of dog can participate in agility. To find an agility class in your area, call the United States Dog Agility Association at (214) 231-9700 They'll also send you a free information package on getting started. Their web site is http:/home.coqui.net/devarona/usdaa3.htm. Because some agility clubs aren't listed with USDAA, you might want to call local kennels, groomers, or veterinarians to find them. If you want more background, The

Dog Agility Page at http://www.dogpatch.org/agility.html provides extensive information for both novices and advanced participants. Here you can find answers to frequently asked questions about the sport, upcoming trials, and agility products and resources. Its best feature is its directory of local clubs that you can search by state. Although it wasn't until 1994 that the American Kennel Club recognized this sport, that organization reports that the response has been tremendous.

Musical Freestyle

Michael Jackson, move over! There's a new dance act in town. In 1991, an owner and her dog stunned the Pacific Canine Showcase with a dance routine that wowed audiences. After putting on a CD, they turned the music up and performed a choreographed obedience routine that had the dog weaving between the owner's legs, bowing, jumping, and making other impressive moves, all in time to the music and in sync with the owner.

By 1994, fun dog lovers with rhythm had formed the Musical Canine Sports International and developed musical freestyle rules and guidelines. Freestyle judges focus on the complexity and originality of routines, as well as the dog's performance. Most routines are a series of the basic obedience commands—heel, down, stay—embellished with spins, weaves, and any other impressive moves the owner can dream up. Big executives at Cycle dog food got wind of this prancing way to do obedience and immediately volun-

teered to sponsor it. In the fall of 1996, the First USA MCSI Cycle Canine Freestyle Competition was held in Eugene, Oregon.

If you think musical freestyle might be your dog activity of choice, the best way to get involved is to join MCSI. For $20, you get a bimonthly *Musical Notes* newsletter and one set of Rules and Judging Guidelines. Because the sport is so new, currently there are no organized classes of musical freestyle. However, several freestyle experts provide demonstrations in cities throughout the U.S. *Musical Notes* lists those seminars and demonstrations. You can also get ideas by ordering one of MCSI's videos of the routines per-

formed at various competitions. To order, write to Ventre Advertising Inc. P. O. Box 350122, Brooklyn, NY 11235.

Musical Freestyle works well with dogs of all breeds as well as mutts. People involved claim it is especially good for older dogs who can no longer compete in rigorous sports like flyball and Frisbee. Dogs who like to show off shine in this sport. If your dog responds to your commands more enthusiastically in front of other dogs or people, you may have a born performer on your hands. One of coauthor Betty Fisher's dogs works best in the show-ring where he knows people are watching him and getting ready to applaud his every move. Even if your dog doesn't live for applause, this sport spices up training and provides motivation for both of you.

If you're the competitive type, rest assured that musical freestyle will have many matches over the next few years. To find out when and where they are, contact Sharon Tutt, MCSI Membership Chairperson at 16665 Parkview Place, Surrey BC, V4N 1Y8, Canada. There is also a great deal of information on the Cycle Canine Freestyle home page at http://www.duke.edu/~awho/fs/frstyl.html.

Ian Dunbar's PuppyDog Allstars K-9 Games

World-renowned animal behaviorist, veterinarian, and author Dr. Ian Dunbar is another who recognized the bored looks on the faces of owners and dogs involved in traditional obedience. He resolved to add some spice to this

necessary training process. The end results were the PuppyDog AllStars K-9 Games where teams of nine owners and their dogs compete for top honors in Musical Chairs, Waltzes with Dogs, Recall Relay, and seven other games. Some of the games are performed with one dog and handler. Others are performed by several dogs and handlers on a team. These games are full of the commands and exercises that go into good obedience training. If you participate in all ten, you'll cover sit, stay, come, down, heeling, the retrieve, and others. Because the games are not too physically demanding, all breeds and ages of dogs can participate.

Fifteen years in the making, the K-9 Games finally debuted in August of 1996. Most of the teams were recruited from obedience schools where trainers could put teams together. However, interested groups can write for the rules and regulations and organize their own teams. Following the guidelines, groups can train together for matches that take place in many cities throughout the United States.

While many have chosen to participate, even more come to watch. Preceding the games, Dr. Ian Dunbar and other experts give lectures on various aspects of dog care. Dr. Dunbar strives to show dog lovers how to help their pets realize their potential in a fun way. For more information, write to Sirius Puppy Training, 2140 Shattuck Avenue, #2406, Berkeley, CA 94704, or phone (707) 745-4237. You can also visit their web site at http://www.puppyworks.com.

Flyball

Dog training can be a lonely activity. After all, the focus must be upon the relationship between the owner and the dog. However, if you get your dog into a team, you have other handlers with whom to commiserate and other pooches to love and encourage.

Official flyball is a relay race with four dogs on a team. The course consists of a starting line, four hurdles, and a flyball box. The first dog leaves his three teammates to jump the hurdles and press the spring-loaded flyball box, which shoots a ball out a short distance. The dog must catch the tennis ball in midair and then run back over the four hurdles. When the first dog recrosses the starting line, the next dog goes. The first team to have all four dogs run without errors wins. The fastest time recorded is 16.9 seconds for a team to run the event. In this sport, the dogs learn how to pay attention, come, retrieve, go, and many other useful exercises.

To provide a competitive medium, the North American Flyball Association, the largest and most respected flyball group, has organized tournaments where teams go through a process of elimination until the best two finally contend. Because of the tournament structure, even the teams that aren't so fast get to participate in at least a few heats.

Since the object is speed, some breeds are more appropriate for flyball than others. The most common breeds participating are: border collies, Labrador retrievers, Doberman pinschers, and Jack Russell terriers. Nevertheless, the NAFA executive director claims that flyball accommodates many

breeds. Yorkshire terriers and Pomeranians have even been known to compete.

Essentially, the dog must be taught to fetch a tennis ball, do a recall, push a pedal, catch the ball, and jump hurdles—once again, a piece of cake for our Caninesteins! Before you get involved in this rigorous sport, make sure your veterinarian gives your dog a clean bill of health.

The North American Flyball Association wrote the regulations and guidelines now used by flyball clubs all over the world. Without a national office, however, it's a little difficult to contact them. They, too, have a web site: http://www.cs.umn.edu/~ianhogg/flyball/flyball.html. For $15 you can receive *Finish Line*, a newsletter which lists all North American teams, tournaments, and events. To start your subscription, send your check to Melanie McAvoy, 2220 W. Albany, Peoria, NY 61604, or E-mail for more information mel.davidson@worldnet.att.net. Another very informative site can be found at: http://dspace.dial.pipex.com/town/square/tac61/flyball.htm.

Frisbee

High-energy dog? Wear him out till even a Big Mac won't get him up on all fours. In traditional Frisbee, the dogs are scored on the number of Frisbees they retrieve and whether all four feet leave the ground. The dog usually must run thirty feet or more before the Frisbee floats to a level where he can snatch it from the air. In freestyle Frisbee, the dog and handler perform a routine to music that incorporates catches and some dance moves. In this entertaining version, the dog jumps from the handler's knee or back and through hoops before a graceful catch. Some dogs even flip before the Frisbee ever threatens to touch the grass. It's all very exciting.

Would your dog be appropriate? Not all dogs are cut out for Frisbee disc training. Some breeds just don't have the physical characteristics to jump and snatch with ease. Basset hounds and bloodhounds don't have the enthusiasm for it, and short-nosed breeds like Boston terriers and English bulldogs just don't have the jaws. The most common dogs seen in Frisbee disc championships are whippets, border collies, Australian cattle dogs, and pointers. However, many other breeds and mixed breeds participate and win high scores. This sport is limited to very healthy dogs with no hip problems. Once again, anyone considering getting involved in Frisbee training should have their dogs examined by their veterinarian. Because of the high, strenuous jumps involved, hips must be monitored carefully.

About ten years after the flying disc was invented in the forties, people began throwing them to their dogs. By the fifties, flying disc competitions

were being held in many locations across the United States. It took the invention of the television set and a whippet named Ashley to really popularize the sport. When news stations broadcast his incredible leaps and tricks, the public was amazed. Seizing a great opportunity, the Friskies Pet-Care Company, makers of Alpo dog food, began sponsoring the competitions that are now called Friskies Alpo Canine Frisbee disc Championships.

Both beginners and experienced dog-owner teams can participate. The series includes community events and regional finals, and culminates with a world finals in Washington, D.C. Any purebred or mixed-breed dog can be entered, regardless of size. There is no entry fee or admission fee. For more information and a current schedule of Alpo Canine Frisbee disc Competitions, send a SASE to:

Peter Bloeme, Director
Alpo Canine Frisbee disc Championships
4060 Peachtree Rd, Ste. 326M
Atlanta, GA 30319

There are also two videos that will help you begin training your dog. *Frisbee Dogs Training Video* and *Frisbee Dogs Throwing Video* is available by calling PRB Associates, Inc. at (800) 786-9240. Good web sites for those interested in Frisbee training are Mary Jo's Frisbee Dog Page at http://www. dogpatch.org/frisbee.html and National Capital Air Canines at http://www.

ais.net/~krobair/ncacinfo.htm. The National Capital Air Canines site contains an extensive section that answers frequently asked questions. You can also actually write to them at NCAC, 2830 Meadow Lane, Falls Church, VA 22042, or call them (703) 532-0709. (If you don't remember those ancient ways of communicating, you can probably find a web site that will give you guidelines on dialing phones and writing letters.)

Therapy Dogs

Medical studies prove that pets lower blood pressure, increase survival rates of heart attack victims, and decrease visits to the doctor. Because of these facts, the Animal Assisted Therapy movement in the United States is growing stronger and stronger. Every week, more hospitals and nursing homes call therapy organizations looking for dogs to come in to entertain and comfort patients. There are hundreds of stories of people reviving from illnesses to say, "Hey! What's slobbering on me?" Often, very elderly folks in nursing homes who won't respond to a nurse or family member will pet and talk to an animal. If your dog never was and never will be a great athlete, training him to be a therapy dog can provide challenge and novelty.

The benefits to the dog are many. As we discussed in Chapter 7, our dogs need jobs! They need to have expectations to meet. Being a therapy dog gives both of you a practical use for all the basic obedience commands. Because you may be called on to work once a week or so, your dog will have

plenty of chances to exercise his new knowledge of commands. He must sit reliably so that he doesn't injure a frail senior citizen. He must heel well as the two of you walk through the busy hospital. He must stay calm and attentive to you even in the presence of distractions and other animals (there may be other therapy dogs there). Beyond the intellectual advantages of learning commands, his rides in the car and immersion in new environments give his brain more opportunities to develop connections and memories.

The best personality profile of a therapy dog is one who is calm but also friendly. Super-friendly, uncontrolled dogs can injure a patient. On the other hand, calm dogs that border on being aloof may not be ideal either. You don't want to have a situation where the cool dog seems to reject a patient longing to pet him. People in hospitals and nursing homes need as many positives as possible. Leave the negatives at home.

Remember, too, sometimes dogs are slapped, poked, and pulled at in therapy situations. Whether this abuse is intentional or accidental, the dog must be immune to it. Further, because a busy hospital is full of loud and sudden noises and movements, the dog must also have an even enough temper to calmly stroll by noisy carts and darting doctors. His understanding of and compliance with your basic obedience commands must be dependable. Urgent and tangible goals like these will motivate you to train consistently and seriously.

You can get your dog started in animal-assisted therapy by contacting The Delta Society, an organization that educates owners and evaluates

potential therapy dogs. When you register, The Delta Society will send you at-home study materials and a list of people who can evaluate your dog. Once your dog is ready, the evaluator will test him to determine how well he handles enthusiastic affection, strangers, noises, and other situations he may encounter in his work as a therapy dog. To find out more about certifying your therapy dog, contact the Delta Society Pet Partners program. Their address and phone are: 289 Perimeter Road, East Renton, WA 98055; (800) 869-6898. Their web site at http://www.deltasociety.org contains lots of information about the program. To find out more basic information, you can fire up the old computer and go to http://www.dog-play.com/therapy. html on the Internet. There, you can search a database of local therapy organizations by state.

In Conclusion...

Because most of these activities are new, they will be getting more and more attention in the years to come. They aim to help dogs reach their potential in a safe, loving environment. Remember, it's only been in this century that pet dogs have outnumbered working dogs (in other words, that the ranks of the canine unemployed have swollen to 90 percent). Because of the dedication of many dog lovers, basic obedience has been extended into novel and exciting ways to turn a bored or misbehaving dog into one that's a joy to be around. Whether your dog is a hypermaniac, a born show-off, or an easy-

going love sponge, an activity exists that fits his personality. These activities nourish his mind, get you involved with other dog people, and open up new doors for both of you.

Now that you're finished with this book, sit down with your heretofore unchallenged dog and inform him that there are going to be some changes in the household. Tell him to take his vitamins because he'll be needing his energy. Play games that make him overcome obstacles and solve problems. Strengthen his memory by asking him to find hidden treats and children. Give him more opportunities to make choices by providing a stimulating environment. While he may never be able to balance the family checkbook, he may learn to pick up his toys, play a little ball, and entertain the kids with hide and seek. Beyond the delight of participating in these challenging games and activities, you'll relish the peace of mind of knowing a helpless creature that is wholly in your care enjoys an engaging life.